SLAVERY

IN THE

WEST INDIES

NEGRO UNIVERSITIES PRESS
NEW YORK

Originally published in 1823, London

Reprinted 1969 by
Negro Universities Press
A DIVISION OF GREENWOOD PUBLISHING CORP.
NEW YORK

Library of Congree Catalogue Card Number 78-82076

SBN 8371-0527-7

PRINTED IN UNITED STATES OF AMERICA

CONTENTS

AN APPEAL

TO THE

RELIGION, JUSTICE, AND HUMANITY

OF

THE INHABITANTS

OF THE

BRITISH EMPIRE,

IN BEHALF OF THE

NEGRO SLAVES IN THE WEST INDIES.

———◆———

BY

WM. WILBERFORCE, ESQ., M.P.

———

Woe unto him that buildeth his house by unrighteousness, and his
chambers by wrong; that useth his neighbour's service without
wages, and giveth him not for his work.   JEREMIAH.

Do justice and love mercy.   MICAH.

———

𝕬 𝔑𝔢𝔴 𝔈𝔡𝔦𝔱𝔦𝔬𝔫.

═══════

A P P E A L,

&c. &c.

To all the inhabitants of the British Empire, who value the favour of God, or are alive to the interests or honour of their country,—to all who have any respect for justice, or any feelings of humanity, I would solemnly address myself. I call upon them, as they shall hereafter answer, in the great day of account, for the use they shall have made of any power or influence with which Providence may have entrusted them, to employ their best endeavours, by all lawful and constitutional means, to mitigate, and, as soon as it may be safely done, to terminate the Negro Slavery of the British Colonies ; a system of the grossest injustice, of the most heathenish irreligion and immorality, of the most unprecedented degradation, and unrelenting cruelty.

At any time, and under any circumstances, from such a heavy load of guilt as this oppression amounts to, it would be our interest no less than our duty to absolve ourselves. But I will not attempt to conceal, that the present embarrassments and distress of our country—a distress, indeed, in which the West Indians themselves have largely participated—powerfully enforce on me the urgency of the obligation under which we lie, to commence, without delay, the preparatory measures for putting an end to a national crime of the deepest moral malignity.

The long continuance of this system, like that of its parent the Slave Trade, can only be accounted for by the generally prevailing ignorance of its real nature, and of its great and numerous evils. Some of the abuses which it involves have indeed been drawn into notice : but when the public attention has been attracted to this subject, it has been unadvisedly turned to particular instances of cruelty, rather than to the system in general, and to those essential and incurable vices which will invariably exist wherever the power of man over man is unlimited. Even at this day, few of our countrymen, comparatively speaking, are at all apprised of the real condition of the bulk of the Negro population ; and, perhaps, many of our non-resident West-Indian proprietors are fully as ignorant of it as other men. Often, indeed, the most humane of the number, (many of them are men whose humanity is unquestionable,) are least of all aware of it, from estimating, not unnaturally, the actual state of the case, by the benevolence of their own well meant, but unavailing, directions to their managers in the western hemisphere.

The persuasion, that it is to the public ignorance of the actual evils of West-Indian Slavery that we can alone ascribe its having been suffered so long to remain unreformed, and almost unnoticed, is strongly confirmed by referring to what passed when the question for abolishing the Slave Trade was seriously debated in 1792. For then, on the general ground merely of the incurable injustice and acknowledged evils of slavery, aggravated, doubtless, by the consideration that it was a slavery forcibly imposed on unoffending men for our advantage, many of the most strenuous and most formidable opponents of the immediate abolition of the Slave Trade charged us with gross inconsistency, in not fairly following up our own arguments, and proposing the gradual extinction also of Slavery itself. "If," they argued, "it is contrary, as you maintain, to the soundest principles of justice, no less than to the clearest dictates of humanity, to permit the seizure, and transportation across the Atlantic, of innocent men to labour for our benefit, can it be more just, or less inhuman, to leave the victims of our rapacity to a life of slavery and degradation, as the hopeless lot of themselves and their descendants for ever? If, indeed, it had been true, as was alleged by the African merchants, that the slaves were only the convicts of Africa, condemned after a fair trial, or that they were delivered by the mercy of their British purchasers from becoming the victims of a bloody superstition, or of a relentless despotism, or of cruel intestine wars,—in short, if, as was urged in defence of the traffic, the situation of the slaves in Africa was so bad that it was worth while, even on the plainest principles of humanity, to bring them away, and to place them in a Christian community, though at the price of all the sufferings they must undergo during the process of their deliverance, yet even then our detaining them as slaves longer than should be necessary for civilizing them, and enabling them to maintain themselves by their own industry, would be indefensible. But when, as we maintained, all these pleas had been proved to be not merely gross falsehoods, but a cruel mockery of the wretched sufferers, how much more strongly were we bound not to desert them so soon as they should be landed in the West Indies, but to provide as early as possible for their deliverance from a bondage which we ourselves declared to have been originally unjust and cruel! But whatever shadow of a plea might have existed for reducing the imported Africans to slavery, surely none could be urged for retaining, in the same hopeless state, their progeny to the latest generation."

Such was, I repeat it, the reasoning of many of our greatest and ablest opponents, as well as of some of our warmest friends. Such, more especially, was the argument of our most powerful antagonist in the House of Commons; and, on these grounds, he, thirty years ago, proposed, that in less than eight years, which of course would have expired at the beginning of the present century, not only should the Slave Trade cease, but the extinction of slavery should itself commence. He proposed, that from that hour every new-born Negro infant should be free; subject only, when he should attain to puberty, to a species of apprenticeship for a few years, to repay the owner for the expense of maintaining him during the period of infancy and boyhood. Can I here forbear remarking, that if the advocates for immediate abolition could have foreseen that the feelings of the House of Commons, then apparently so warmly excited, and so resolutely fixed on the instant extinction of the Slave Trade, would so soon subside into a long and melancholy apathy ; and had they in consequence acceded to these proposals, the Slavery of the West Indies would by this time nearly have expired, and we should be now rejoicing in the delightful change which the mass of our Negro population would have experienced, from a state of ignominious bondage to the condition of a free and happy peasantry.

And by whom was this proposal made? Was it by some hot-headed enthusiast, some speculative votary of the rights of man? No : by the late Lord Melville, then Mr. Dundas, a statesman of many great and rare endowments, of a vigorous intellect, and superior energy of mind ; but to whom no one ever imputed an extravagant zeal for speculative rights or modern theories. And let it be taken into account in what character he suggested this measure. In that which seemed to give a pledge not only for its justice but for its expediency ;—that of the partizan and acknowledged patron of the West-Indian body ; and at the very moment when he was most conversant with all their affairs, and naturally most alive to all their interests. If any emotions of surprise, therefore, should be excited by my present Appeal, it should be, that it has been so long delayed, rather than that it is now brought forward ; that, previously to our commencing our endeavours for the mitigation and ultimate extinction of slavery, we should have suffered twenty-two long years to elapse, beyond that interval for notice and preparation, which even the advocate of the West Indians himself had voluntarily proposed, as what appeared to him at once safe and reasonable.

It is due also to the character of the late Mr. Burke to state, that long before the subject of the Slave Trade had engaged the public attention, his large and sagacious mind, though far from being fully informed of the particulars of the West-Indian system, had become sensible of its deeply

criminal nature. He had even devised a plan for ameliorating, and by degrees putting an end both to the Slave
Trade and to the state of slavery itself in the West Indies. He proposed, by education, and, above all, by religious instruction, to prepare the poor degraded slaves for
the enjoyment of civil rights; taking them, in the mean
time, into the guardianship and superintendence of officers
to be appointed by the British Government. It scarcely
needs be remarked, in how great a degree Mr. Burke was
an enemy to all speculative theories ; and his authority will
at least absolve those who now undertake the cause of the
Negro Slaves, from the imputation of harshly and unwar-
rantably disturbing a wholesome and legitimate system of
civil subordination.

But if such were the just convictions produced in the
mind of Mr. Burke, though very imperfectly acquainted
with the vices of the West-India system—still more, if it
was conceded by many of those who opposed the immediate abolition of the Slave Trade, more especially by that
politic statesman, Mr. Dundas, that a state of slavery, considered merely as a violation of the natural rights of human beings, being unjust in its origin, must be unwarrantable in its continuance—what would have been the
sentiments and feelings produced in all generous and
humane minds by our West-Indian Slavery, had they known
the detail of its great and manifold evils ?

The importance of proving, that the alleged decrease of
the slaves arose from causes which it was in the master's
power easily to remove, led the Abolitionists of the Slave
Trade, in stating the actual vices of the West-Indian system, to dwell much, and too exclusively, perhaps, on the
slaves being under-fed and over-worked, and on the want
of due medical care and medical comforts. These evils,
which are indeed very great, must, of course, be aggravated where the planters were in embarrassed circumstances, notoriously the situation of the greater part of the
owners of West-Indian estates. But, speaking generally,
there exists essentially in the system itself, from various

causes, a natural tendency towards the maximum of labour, and the minimum of food and other comforts. That such was the case in general, whatever exceptions there might be in particular instances, was decisively established by the testimony even of West-Indian authorities; and it was fatally confirmed by the decrease of the slaves in almost all our settlements. No other satisfactory explanation could be given of this melancholy fact; for it is contrary to universal experience as to the Negro race, not in their own country only, where they are remarkably prolific, but in the case of the domestic slaves, even in our Sugar Colonies. The free Negroes and Mulattoes, and also the Maroons*, in the island of Jamaica, the Charaibs† of St. Vincent, and the Negroes of Bencoolen, were all known to increase their numbers, though under circumstances far from favourable to population; and, above all, a striking contrast was found in the rapid native increase of the Negro Slaves in the United States of America, though situated in a climate far less suited to the Negro constitution than that of the West Indies. There alone, in a climate much the same as that of Africa, it was declared impossible even to keep up their numbers, without continual importations. This fact alone was a strong presumptive proof, and was raised by various concurrent facts and arguments into a positive certainty, that the decrease of the slaves arose in no small degree, not only from an excess of labour, but from the want of a requisite supply of food, and of other necessaries and comforts. The same phenomena, I fear, are still found to exist, and to indicate the continuance of the same causes. For unless I am much misinformed, there is still a progressive decrease by mortality in most of our Colonies; and if in a smaller ratio to their

---

* The descendants of the Negro Slaves who fled into the woods, when Jamaica was taken by Venables and Vernon, under Oliver Cromwell, and who, about eighty years ago, were settled in separate villages as free Negroes.

† The descendants of the crew of an African ship which was wrecked on the island about a century ago.

whole population than formerly, it is to be remembered
that the enormous loss, in the seasoning of newly imported
Africans, now no longer aggravates the sad account.

But though the evils which have been already enume-
rated are of no small amount, in estimating the physical
sufferings of human beings, especially of the lower rank,
yet, to a Christian eye, they shrink almost into insigni-
ficance when compared with the moral evils that remain
behind—with that, above all, which runs through the whole
of the various cruel circumstances of the Negro Slave's
condition, and is at once the effect of his wrongs and sufferings, their bitter aggravation, and the pretext for their
continuance,—his extreme degradation in the intellectual
and moral scale of being, and in the estimation of his White
oppressors.

The proofs of the extreme degradation of the slaves, in
the latter sense, are innumerable; and indeed it must be
confessed, that in the minds of Europeans in general, more
especially in vulgar minds, whether vulgar from the want
of education, or morally vulgar, (a more inwrought and
less curable vulgarity,) the personal peculiarities of the
Negro race could scarcely fail, by diminishing sympathy,
to produce impressions, not merely of contempt, but even
of disgust and aversion. But how strongly are these impressions sure to be confirmed and augmented, when to
all the effects of bodily distinctions are superadded all
those arising from the want of civilization and knowledge,
and still more, all the hateful vices that slavery never fails
to engender or to aggravate. Such, in truth, must naturally be the effect of these powerful causes, that even the
most ingeniously constructed system which humanity and
policy combined could have devised, would in vain have
endeavoured to counteract them: how much more powerfully then must they operate, especially in low and unedu-
cated minds, when the whole system abounds with institutions and practices which tend to confirm and strengthen
their efficiency, and to give to a contemptuous aversion for
the Negro race the sanction of manners and of law.

It were well if the consequences of these impressions were only to be discovered among the inferior ranks of the privileged class, or only to be found in the opinions and conduct of individuals. But in the earlier laws of our colonies they are expressed in the language of insult, and in characters of blood. And too many of these laws still remain unrepealed, to permit the belief that the same odious spirit of legislation no longer exists, or to relieve the injured objects of them from their degrading influence. The slaves were systematically depressed below the level of human beings*. And though I confess, that it is of less concern to a slave, under what laws he lives, than what is the character of his master, yet if the laws had extended to them favour and protection instead of degradation, this would have tended to raise them in the social scale, and, operating insensibly on the public mind, might, by degrees, have softened the extreme rigour of their bondage. Such, however, had been the contrary effects of an opposite process, on the estimation of the Negro race, before the ever-to-be-honoured Granville Sharpe, and his followers, had begun to vindicate their claim to the character and privileges of human nature, that a writer of the highest authority on all West-India subjects, Mr. Long, in his celebrated History of Jamaica, though pointing out some of the particulars of their ill treatment, scrupled not to state it as his opinion, that in the gradations of being, Negroes were little elevated above the oran outang, " that type of man." Nor was this an unguarded or a hastily thrown-out assertion. He institutes a laborious comparison of the Negro race with that species of baboon; and declares, that, "lu-

---

* An act of Barbadoes (8th Aug. 1688,) prescribing the mode of trial of slaves, recites, that "they being brutish slaves, deserve not, for the baseness of their condition, to be tried by the legal trial of twelve men of their peers, &c." Another clause of the same act, speaks of the "barbarous, wild, and savage natures of the same Negroes and other slaves," being such as renders them wholly unqualified to be governed by the laws, practices, and customs of other nations. Other instances of a like spirit might be cited in the acts of other colonies.

dicrous as the opinion may seem, he does not think that an oran outang husband would be any dishonour to a Hottentot female." When we find such sentiments as these to have been unblushingly avowed by an author of the highest estimation among the West-India colonists, we are prepared for what we find to have been, and, I grieve to say, still continues to be, the practical effects of these opinions.

The first particular of subsisting legal oppression that I shall notice, and which is at once a decisive proof of the degradation of the Negro race, in the eyes of the Whites, and a powerful cause of its continnance, is of a deeply rooted character, and often productive of the most cruel effects. In the contemplation of law they are not persons, but mere chattels; and as such are liable to be seized and sold by creditors and by executors, in payment of their owner's debts; and this separately from the estates on which they are settled. By the operation of this system, the most meritorious slave who may have accumulated a little peculium, and may be living with his family in some tolerable comfort, who by long and faithful services may have endeared himself to his proprietor or manager—who, in short, is in circumstances that mitigate greatly the evils of his condition—is liable at once to be torn for ever from his home, his family, and his friends, and to be sent to serve a new master, perhaps in another island, for the rest of his life.

Another particular of their degradation by law, which, in its effects, most perniciously affects their whole civil condition, and of which their inadequate legal protection is a sure and necessary consequence, is their evidence being inadmissible against any free person. The effect of this cannot be stated more clearly or compendiously than in the memorable evidence of a gentleman eminently distinguished for the candour with which he gave to the Slave-Trade Committee the result of his long personal experience in the West Indies,—the late Mr. Otley, Chief-justice of St. Vincent's, himself a planter:—"As the evidence of

Slaves is never admitted against White men, the difficulty of legally establishing the facts is so great, that White men are in a manner put beyond the reach of the law." It is due also to the late Sir William Young, long one of the most active opponents of the abolition, to state, that he likewise, when Governor of Tobago, acknowledged, as a radical defect in the administration of justice, that the law of evidence " covered the most guilty European with impunity."

The same concession was made by both houses of the legislature of Grenada, in the earliest inquiries of the Privy Council. The only difficulty, as they stated, that had been found in putting an effectual stop to gross and wanton cruelty towards slaves, was that of bringing home the proof of the fact against the delinquent by satisfactory evidence, those who were capable of the guilt, being in general artful enough to prevent any but slaves being witnesses of the fact. " As the matter stands," they add, " though we hope the instances in this island are at this day not frequent, yet it must be admitted with regret, that the persons prosecuted, and who certainly were guilty, have escaped for want of legal proof."

It is obvious that the same cause must produce the same effect in all our other slave colonies, although there has not been found the same candour in confessing it.

The next evil which I shall specify, for which the extreme degradation of these poor beings, in the eyes of their masters, can alone account, is the driving system. Not being supposed capable of being governed like other human beings, by the hope of reward, or the fear of punishment, they are subjected to the immediate impulse or present terror of the whip, and are driven at their work like brute animals. Lower than this it is scarcely possible for man to be depressed by man. If such treatment does not find him vile and despised, it must infallibly make him so. Let it not however be supposed, that the only evil of this truly odious system is its outraging the moral character of the human species, or its farther degrading the slaves in the eyes of all who are in authority over them, and thereby extinguishing that sympathy which would be their best protection. The whip is itself a dreadful instrument of punishment; and the mode of inflicting that punishment shockingly indecent and degrading. The drivers themselves, commonly, or rather always slaves, are usually the strongest and stoutest of the Negroes; and though they are forbidden to give more than a few lashes at a time, as the immediate chastisement of faults committed at their work, yet the power over the slaves which they thus possess unavoidably invests them with a truly formidable tyranny, the consequences of which, to the unfortunate subjects of it, are often in the highest degree oppressive and pernicious. No one who reflects on the subject can be at a loss to anticipate one odious use which is too commonly made of this despotism, in extorting, from the fears of the young females who are subject to it, compliances with the licentious desires of the drivers, which they might otherwise have refused from attachment to another, if not from moral feelings and restraints. It is idle and insulting to talk of improving the condition of these poor beings, as rational and moral agents, while they are treated in a manner which precludes self-government, and annihilates all human motives but such as we impose on a maniac, or on a hardened and incorrigible convict.

Another abuse, which shews, like the rest, the extreme degradation of the Negro race, and the apathy which it creates in their masters, is the cruel, and, at least in the case of the female sex, highly indecent punishments inflicted in public, and in the face of day, often in the presence of the gang, or of the whole assembled population of an estate. From their low and ignominious condition it doubtless proceeds, that they are in some degree regarded as below the necessity of observing towards others the proper decencies of life, or of having those decencies observed by others towards them.

It is no doubt also chiefly owing to their not being yet

raised out of that extreme depth in which they are sunk, so much below the level of the human species, that no attempts have been made to introduce among them the Christian institution of marriage, that blessed union which the Almighty himself established as a fundamental law at the creation of man, to be as it were the well-spring of all the charities of life—the source of all domestic comfort and social improvement—the moral cement of civilized society.

In truth, so far have the masters been from attempting to establish marriage generally among their slaves. that even the idea of its introduction among them never seems to have seriously suggested itself to their minds. In the commencement of the long contest concerning the abolition of the Slave Trade, it was one of a number of questions respecting the treatment of slaves in the West Indies put by the Privy Council, " What is the practice respecting the marriage of Negro Slaves, and what are the regulations concerning it ? " In all instances, and from every colony, the answers returned were such as these : " They do not marry." " They cohabit by mutual consent," &c. " If by marriage is meant a regular contract and union of one man with one woman, enforced by positive institutions, no such practice exists among the slaves, and they are left entirely free in this respect," &c.

Let me not be supposed ignorant of some acts of the West-Indian Legislatures, the perusal of which might produce an opposite impression on the uninformed and credulous, as they gravely require all owners, managers, &c. of slaves, under a penalty, to *exhort* their slaves to receive the ceremony of marriage as instituted under the forms of the Christian religion : they even profess " *to protect the domestic and connubial happiness of slaves.*" But, in direct contradiction to the impression that would naturally be produced by these laws, the Privy Council, but a year after their enactment, was informed, in express terms, that in the very island in which these laws had been passed, there was no such thing as marriage, except that sometimes it existed among the Roman-Catholic Slaves. This neglect of marriage is the more extraordinary, because the owners of slaves are powerfully called on by self-interest, no less than by religion and humanity, to make the attempt to promote it. With one concurrent voice they have spoken of the licentiousness of the slaves, and of the numerous bad consequences which follow from the promiscuous intercourse so generally prevalent between the sexes. To this cause, indeed, they chiefly ascribed that inability to keep up the numbers of their slaves which they credibly professed to lament most deeply. How strange, then, that the very institution with which the Almighty associated the primeval command, "Increase and multiply," seems not even to have presented itself to their minds. I have scarcely found a solitary instance in which the want of marriage is regretted, or specified as in any degree instrumental in preventing the natural increase of slaves, which was desired so earnestly. I recollect not a word having been seriously stated on the subject, until long after the charge of neglecting the marriage institution had been strongly urged against the slave-owners by the Abolitionists. Then, indeed, it was stated in the Meliorating Act of the Leeward Islands of 1798, that it was unnecessary, and even improper, to enforce the celebration of any religious rites among the slaves, in order to sanctify contracts, the faithful performance of which could be looked for only by a regular improvement in religion, morality, and civilization. To those who know any thing of the public mind in our West-Indian Colonies, this passage speaks very intelligible language. It plainly intimates the very position I have been laying down, that the slaves are considered as too degraded to be proper subjects for the marriage institution. A striking corroboration of this position was afforded but a few years ago, when a very worthy clergyman, in one of our Leeward Islands, having obtained the master's leave, proposed to solemnize the marriage of a slave according to the forms of the Church of England. The publication of the banns produced an universal ferment in the colony: the case was immediately referred to the highest legal authorities upon the spot ; nor was the question as a point of law settled until it had been referred to his Majesty's legal advisers in this country.

I have dwelt the longer, and insisted the more strongly on the universal want of the marriage institution among the slaves, because, among the multiplied abuses of the West-Indian system, it appears to me to be one of the most influential in its immoral and degrading effects. It should, however, be remarked, that though the prevalence of promiscuous intercourse between the male and female slaves is nearly universal, yet mutual and exclusive, though rarely permanent, attachments between two individuals of different sexes frequently take place ; and as the Africans notoriously have warm affections, the regard is often very strong, so long as it continues. On the mother's side also the instincts of nature are too sure not to produce great affection for her children, some degree of which also will often be found in the father. But how far are these precarious connections from producing that growing attachment, that mutual confidence, which spring from an identity of interest, from the common feeling for a common progeny, with all the multiplied emotions of hope and even of fear, of joys and even of sorrows, which bind families together, when mutually attached to each other by the indissoluble bonds of a Christian union ? Alas ! the injustice with which these poor creatures are treated accompanies them throughout the whole of their progress ; and even the cordial drops which a gracious Providence has elsewhere poured into the cup of poverty and labour, are to them vitiated and embittered.

It must also be observed, that licentiousness thus produced is not confined to the Negroes. The fact is perfectly notorious, that it has been the general policy to employ, instead of married managers and overseers, single young men, as the immediate superintendents of the gangs ; and hence it too naturally follows, that they who, from their being the depositories of the master's authority, ought to be the protectors of the purity of the young females, too often become their corrupters.

It is a farther important truth, pregnant with the most serious consequences, that the extreme degradation which is supposed to render the slaves unfit to form the marriage contract, belongs not merely to their situation as slaves, but to their colour as Negroes. Hence it adheres not only to those who are for ever released from slavery, but to those also who, by having one European parent, might be presumed to be raised highly above the level of the servile race. Such is the incurable infamy inherent in what still belongs to them of African origin, that they are at an almost immeasurable distance in the scale of being below the lowest of the Whites*. The free Women of Colour

* The extreme degradation of the coloured race, as it affects their marriage relations, is strikingly illustrated by a passage in one of the many pamphlets published against the Registry Bill, in 1816, by a gentleman some time resident in Barbadoes. He speaks with real humanity of the Free Coloured People, and strongly recommends their being invested with civil and political rights. Such is the uncommon enlargement of his mind, that he even suggests a plan, through the medium of a moral union of the sexes among the Coloured People in the Colonies, for the gradual emancipation of the slaves; yet he very strongly deprecates any attempt to introduce any such connection between them and the White inhabitants : and he owns that the West-Indian prejudice is sufficiently implanted in his own mind, to render such a connection not only repugnant to his feelings, but " contrary to his idea of morals, religion, and polity." Observe here, that this West-Indian prejudice is only against a _moral_ union and connection; for he actually informs us, that the _immoral_ connection with this de-graded class of the female population is almost universal, prevailing, with scarcely an exception, among the married no less than the un-married men. He states, and it is abundantly confirmed by Mr. Ed-wards, that prostitution is unhappily now the only portion of the Coloured women; and that the White men who form connections with them purchase them of their owners, and in many instances of their own parents. But against the _moral_ union he declares that he would guard, by advising that the laws should be made to attach the _heaviest pains and penalties of a felonious act_ upon the parties so intermarrying. The opinion of a single individual, however respectable, would scarcely have sufficient weight to entitle him to so much notice in any general argument concerning the treatment of the Negroes ; but it becomes

deem an illicit connection with a White man more respectable than a legal union with a Coloured husband ; while
the Mulatto males, as Mr. B. Edwards declares with great
feeling, are unhappily in too low a state of degradation to
think of matrimony. Well may he then remark, that
their spirits seem to sink under the consciousness of their
condition *. Thus a fatal looseness of principle and practice diffuses itself throughout the whole community. A
licentious intercourse between the White men and the
Coloured females was confessed by Mr. Long to be general
in his day ; and Mr. B. Edwards, whose History was published so recently as 1793, while he expresses himself with
great pity for the wretched victims of this dissoluteness,
acknowledges that the general morals were then little, if
at all improved, in this particular.

Nor let this be deemed a consideration of subordinate
importance. A most sagacious observer of human nature,
the late Dr. Paley, states,—" It is a fact, however it be
accounted for," that " the criminal commerce of the sexes
corrupts and depraves the mind and moral character more
than any single species of vice whatsoever." " These
indulgences," he adds, " in low life, are usually the first
stage in men's progress to the most desperate villainies ;
and in high life to that lamented dissoluteness of principle
which manifests itself in a profligacy of public conduct,
and a contempt of the obligations of religion and moral
probity." This cannot be surprising to any considerate
mind. The Supreme Ordainer of all things, in his moral
administration of the universe, usually renders crime, in
the way of natural consequences, productive of punishment ;

of real importance when, as in this instance, an advocate for the
West-Indian cause bears his testimony to the generally prevailing sen-
timents and practices in one of the largest and most ancient of our
West-Indian colonies.

* Can I forbear adding, that Mr. Edwards states, that to the Negroes
these poor degraded Mulattoes are objects of envy and hatred, for the
supposed superiority of their condition? How low then must the
former be sunk in the scale of being !

and it surely was to be expected that he would manifest, by some strong judicial sanction, his condemnation of practices which are at war with the marriage institution,— the great expedient for maintaining the moral order and social happiness of mankind.

In my estimate of things, however, and I trust in that of the bulk of my countrymen, though many of the physical evils of our colonial slavery are cruel, and odious, and pernicious, the almost universal destitution of religious and moral instruction among the slaves is the most serious of all the vices of the West-Indian system ; and had there been no other, this alone would have most powerfully enforced on my conscience the obligation of publicly declaring my decided conviction, that it is the duty of the legislature of this country to interpose for the mitigation and future termination of a state in which the ruin of the moral man, if I may so express myself, has been one of the sad consequences of his bondage.

It cannot be denied, I repeat, that the slaves, more especially the great body of the field Negroes, are practi- cally strangers to the multiplied blessings of the Christian Revelation.

What a consideration is this ! A nation, which, besides the invaluable benefit of an unequalled degree of true civil liberty, has been favoured with an unprecedented measure of religious light, with its long train of attendant blessings, has been for two centuries detaining in a state of slavery, beyond example rigorous, and, in some particulars, worse than Pagan darkness and depravity, hundreds of thousands of their fellow-creatures, originally torn from their native land by fraud and violence. Generation after generation have thus been pining away ; and in this same condition of ignorance and degradation they still, for the most part, remain. This I am well aware is an awful charge ; but it undeniably is too well founded, and scarcely admits of any exception beyond what has been effected by those excel- lent, though too commonly traduced and persecuted, men, the Christian Missionaries. They have done all that it has been possible for them to do; and, through the Divine blessing, they have indeed done much, especially in the towns, and among the household slaves, considering the many and great obstacles with which they have had to contend.

I must not be supposed ignorant that of late years various colonial laws have been passed, professedly with a view to the promoting of religion among the slaves: but they are all, I fear, worse than nullities. In truth, the solicitude which they express for the personal protection, and still more for the moral interests, of the slaves, contrasted with the apparent forgetfulness of those interests which so generally follows in the same community, might have appeared inexplicable, but for the frank declaration of the Governor of one of the West-Indian islands, which stood among the foremost in passing one of these boasted laws for ameliorating the condition of the slaves. That law contained clauses which, with all due solemnity, and with penalties for the non-observance of its injunctions, prescribed the religious instruction of the slaves; and the promoting of the marriage institution among them; and in order " to secure as far as possible the good treatment of the slaves, and to ascertain the cause of their decrease, if any," it required certificates of the slaves' increase and decrease to be annually delivered on oath, under a penalty of 50l. currency. His Majesty's Government, some time after, very meritoriously wishing for information as to the state of the slaves, applied to the Governor for some of the intelligence which this act was to provide. To this application the Governor, the late Sir George Prevost, replied as follows: " The Act of the Legislature, entitled 'An Act for the Encouragement, Protection, and better Government of Slaves,' appears to have been considered, from the day it was passed until this hour, as a political measure to avert the interference of the mother country in the management of slaves." The same account of the motives by which the legislatures of other West-Indian islands were induced to pass acts for ameliorating the condition of the Slaves, was given by several of the witnesses who were examined in the committee of the House of Commons in 1790 and 1791.

In all that I state concerning the religious interests of the slaves, as well as in every other instance, I must be understood to speak only of the *general* practice. There are, I know, resident in this country, individual owners of slaves, and some, as I believe, even in the colonies, who have been sincerely desirous that their slaves should enjoy the blessings of Christianity : though often, I lament to say, where they have desired it, their pious endeavours have been of little or no avail;—so hard is it, especially for absent proprietors, to stem the tide of popular feeling and practice, which sets strongly in every colony against the religious instruction of slaves ;—so hard also, I must add, is it to reconcile the necessary means of such instruction with the harsh duties and harsher discipline to which these poor beings are subjected. The gift even of the rest of the Sabbath is more than the established œconomics of a sugar plantation permit even the most independent planter to confer, while the law tacitly sanctions its being wholly withheld from them.

Generally speaking, throughout the whole of our West-Indian islands, the field slaves, or common labourers, instead of being encouraged or even permitted to devote the Sunday to religious purposes, are employed either in working their provision-grounds for their own and their families' subsistence, or are attending, often carrying heavy oads to, the Sunday markets, which frequently, in Jamaica, are from ten to fifteen miles distant from their abodes.

These abuses confessedly continue to prevail in despite of the urgent remonstrances, for more than the last half century, of members of the colonial body ; and these sometimes, like Mr. B. Edwards, the most accredited advocates for the interests and character of the West Indians.

The insensibility of the planters, even to the temporal

good effects of Christianity on their slaves, is the more surprising, because, besides their having been powerfully enforced by self-interest, as I have already stated, in restraining a licentious intercourse between the sexes, they were strongly recommended, especially in the great island of Jamaica, by another consideration of a very peculiar nature. The Jamaica planters long imputed the most injurious effects on the health and even the lives of their slaves, to the African practice of Obeah, or witch-craft. The agents for Jamaica declared to the Privy Council, in 1788, that they " ascribed a very considerable portion of the annual mortality among the Negroes in that island to that fascinating mischief." I know that of late, ashamed of being supposed to have punished witchcraft with such severity, it has been alleged, that the professors of Obeah used to prepare and administer poison to the subjects of their spells : but any one who will only examine the laws of Jamaica against these practices, or read the evidence of the agents, will see plainly that this was not the view that was taken of the proceedings of the Obeah-men, but that they were considered as impostors, who preyed on their ignorant countrymen by a pretended in-tercourse with evil spirits, or by some other pretences to supernatural powers. The idea of rooting out any form of pagan superstition by severity of punishment, especially in wholly uninstructed minds, like that of extirpating Christianity by the fire and the fagot, has long been exploded among the well-informed ; and it has even been established, that the devilish engine of persecution recoils back on its employers, and disseminates the very principles it would suppress. Surely then it might have been expected, that, if from no other motive, yet for the pur-pose of rooting a pagan superstition out of the minds of the slaves, the aid of Christianity would have been called in, as the safest species of knowledge : and it was strange if the Jamaica gentlemen were ignorant of the indubitable fact, that Christianity never failed to chase away these vain terrors of darkness and Paganism.

No sooner did a Negro become a Christian, than the Obeah-man despaired of bringing him into subjection. And it is well worthy of remark, that when in the outset of our abolition proceedings, his Majesty's Privy Council, among a number of queries sent out to the different West-India islands, concerning the condition of the slaves, had proposed several concerning the nature and effects of this African superstition, of which the Privy Council had heard so much from the agents for Jamaica, the Council and Assembly of the island of Antigua, in which, through the successful labours of the Moravian and Methodist missionaries, great numbers of the slaves had become Christians, resented, as an imputation on their understandings, the very idea of their being supposed to have considered the practices of the Obeah-men as deserving of any serious attention. Surely then we might have expected that regard for the temporal well-being of the slaves, if not for their highest interests, would have prompted their owners to endeavour to bring them out of their present state of religious darkness into the blessed light of Christianity. But even self-interest itself appears to lose its influence, when it is to be promoted by means of introducing Christianity among the slaves.

If any thing were wanting to add the last finishing tint to the dark colouring of this gloomy picture, it would be afforded by a consideration which still remains behind. However humiliating the statement must be to that legislature which exercises its superintendency over every part of the British Empire; it is nevertheless true, that, low in point of morals as the Africans may have been in their own country, their descendants, who have never seen the continent of Africa, but who are sprung from those who for several successive generations have been resident in the Christian colonies of Great Britain, are still lower. Nay, they are universally represented as remarkable in those colonies for vices which are directly opposite to the character which has been given of the Africans by several of the most intelligent travellers who have visited the interior

of their native country. In proof of this assertion, I refer
not to any delineations of the African character by what
might be supposed to be partial hands. Let any one pe-
ruse the writings of authors who opposed the abolition of
the Slave Trade ; more especially the Travels of Mr. Parke
and M. Golberry, both published since the commencement of the Slave-Trade contest. It is not unworthy of
remark, that many of the Africans in their own country
are raised, by not being altogether illiterate, far above the
low level to which the entire want of all education de-
presses the field slaves in the West Indies. It is stated
by Mr. Parke, who took his passage from Africa to the
West Indies in a slave-ship, that of one hundred and thirty
slaves which the vessel conveyed, about twenty-five of
them, who, as he supposes, had been of free condition,
could most of them write a little Arabic. The want, however, of this measure of literature is of small account ;
but compare the moral nature of the Africans, while yet
living in their native land, and in all the darkness and
abominations of Paganism, with the character universally
given of the same Africans in our West-Indian colonies.
He will find that the Negroes, who while yet in Africa
were represented to be industrious, generous, eminent for
truth, seldom chargeable with licentiousness, distinguished
for their domestic affections, and capable at times of acts
of heroic magnanimity, are described as being in the West
Indies the very opposite in all particulars ; selfish, indolent,
deceitful, ungrateful,—and above all, in whatever respects
the intercourse between the sexes, incurably licentious.

And now, without a farther or more particular delineation of the slavery of the British colonies, what a system
do we behold ! Is it too much to affirm, that there never
was, certainly never before in a Christian country, a mass
of such aggravated enormities ?

That such a system should so long have been suffered to
exist in any part of the British Empire will appear, to our
posterity, almost incredible. It had, indeed, been less
surprising, if its seat had been in regions, like those of

Hindostan, for instance, where a vast population had come into our hands in all the full-blown enormity of heathen institutions ; where the bloody superstitions, and the un-natural cruelties and immoralities of Paganism, had esta-blished themselves in entire authority, and had produced their natural effects in the depravity and moral degradation of the species ; though even in such a case as that, our excuse would hold good no longer than for the period which might be necessary for reforming the native abuses by those mild and reasonable means which alone are acknowledged to be just in principle, or practically effec-tual to their purpose   But that in communities formed from their very origin by a Christian people, and in colo-nies containing no Pagan inhabitants but those whom we ourselves have compulsorily brought into it,—inhabitants too, who, from all the circumstances of their case, had the strongest possible claims on us, both for the reparation of their wrongs, and the relief of their miseries,—such a sys-tem should have been continued for two centuries, and by a people who may, nevertheless, I trust, be affirmed to be the most moral and humane of nations, is one of those anomalies which, if it does not stagger the belief, will at least excite the astonishment of future ages.

But it may naturally, and perhaps not unfairly, be asked of the Abolitionists—You professed to be well acquainted with the state of things in the West Indies when you moved for the abolition of the Slave Trade : if you then thought the system to be at all such as you now state it to be, how could you rest contented with restricting your efforts to the abolition of the traffic in slaves, contrary, as you confess, to the wishes and even the endeavours of many friends of your great cause, and of some even of its enemies ?

It is true, that the evils of the West-Indian system had not passed unnoticed ; and we would gladly have brought forward a plan for ameliorating the condition of the Ne-groes, but that the effort was beyond our strength.   We found the adversaries of the abolition far too numerous and too powerful for us, and we were perfectly sure that we should greatly add to their number and vehemence by striking also at the system of slavery. But farther I will frankly confess, that we greatly deceived ourselves by expecting much more benefit to the plantation Negroes from the abolition of the Slave Trade than has actually resulted from that measure. We always relied much on its efficiency in preparing the way for a general emancipation of the slaves: for let it be remembered, that, from the very first, Mr. Pitt, Mr. Fox, Lord Grenville, Lord Lansdowne, Lord Grey, and all the rest of the earliest Abolitionists, declared that the extinction of slavery was our great and ultimate object ; and we trusted, that by compelling the planters to depend wholly on native increase for the supply of their gangs, they would be forced to improve the condition of their slaves, to increase their food, to lessen their labour, to introduce task-work, to abolish the driving system, together with degrading and indecent punishments, to attach the slaves to the soil, and, with proper qualifications, to admit their testimony as witnesses —a necessary step to all protection by law ; above all, to attend to their religious and moral improvement, and to one of the grand peculiarities of Christianity, the marriage institution. By the salutary operation of these various improvements, the slaves would have become qualified for the enjoyment of liberty ; and preparation would have been made for that happy day, when the yoke should be taken off for ever, when the blessed transmutation should take place of a degraded slave population into a free and industrious peasantry*.

---

* It is the more necessary to state, that the views of the Abolitionists were always directed towards the extinction of slavery, after preparing the Black population for the enjoyment of it ; because, from some statements which were made in the Register-bill controversy, we may expect that our opponents will renew the charge they then brought against us, that we had originally disclaimed all views of emancipating the slaves actually in the islands, confining ourselves exclusively to the prohibition of all future importations of Negroes. Our explanation is

We were too sanguine in our hopes as to the effects of the abolition in our colonies ; we judged too favourably of human nature ; we thought too well of the colonial assemblies ; we did not allow weight enough to the effects of rooted prejudice, and inveterate habits—to absenteeship, a vice which, taken in its whole extent, is perhaps one of the most injurious of the whole system ; to the distressed finances of the planters ; and, above all, to the effects of the extreme degradation of the Negro slaves, and to the long and entire neglect of Christianity among them, with all its attendant blessings.

True it is, that from the want of effectual Register Acts, the experiment has not been fairly tried ; as the abolition is in consequence known to be a law that may easily be

clear and short. Our opponents imputed to us that our real intention was, immediately, to emancipate the slave population of the Colonies : they were aware that there were many who felt themselves bound by the most urgent principles of justice and humanity, at once to put an end to a system of crimes, which was so falsely called a trade in Negroes, who yet would oppose all endeavours to emancipate the slaves without those previous and preparatory measures that would be requisite for enabling them to render the acquisition of liberty either safe for their owners or beneficial to themselves We, in consequence, declared, that although we certainly did look forward ultimately to the emancipation of the slaves, yet that the object we were then pursuing was only the abolition of the Slave Trade, of which it was one grand recommendation, that, by stopping the further influx of uncivilized Africans, and by rendering the planters sensible that they must in future depend on the native increase for keeping up their slave population, it would tend powerfully to prepare the way for the great and happy change of slave into free labourers. Our adversaries, however, continuing artfully to confound abolition and emancipation, our efforts were often employed in distinguishing between the two, and in distinctly and fully explaining our real meaning ; nor am I conscious of any occasion, on which we disclaimed the intention of emancipation, without accompanying the disclaimer with the clear explanation that it was immediate, not ultimate emancipation, which we disclaimed. Not to mention declarations without number of our real meaning, various illustrations might be referred to of the chief speakers in those debates, which would prove that the emancipation of the slaves was the ultimate, though not the immediate, object of all those who took the lead as advocates for the abolition of the Slave Trade.

evaded. For, let it be ever borne in mind, that the ground of our persuasion was, that the absolute prohibition of all future importation of slaves into the colonies, provided means were adopted for insuring its permanent execution, would exercise a sort of moral compulsion over the minds of the planters, and even of their managers and overseers, and induce them, for the necessary end of maintaining the Black population, to adopt effectual measures for reforming the principal abuses of the system ; but it is manifest, that such compulsion could not arise from a law which they had power to elude at pleasure. I am willing, however, for my own part, to admit that this foundation-stone of our hopes may have rested on sandy ground ; for what has since passed has proved to me how little prudence and foresight can effect in opposition to the stubborn prejudices, and strong passions, and inveterate habits that prevail in our West-Indian assemblies. With one single exception in favour of the free Coloured People in Jamaica, the admission of their evidence, which, however, only placed them in the situation which they had always before occupied in most of our other islands, I know not any vice of the system that has been rooted out, any material improvement that has been adopted. Not only the abuses which had been pointed out by the Abolitionists are still existing in all their original force, but some of those reforms which had been urged on the colonial legislatures by their warmest friends and most approved advocates remain to this hour unadopted in every island. Mr. B. Edwards, for instance, nearly thirty years ago, in his History of the West Indies, recommended the introduction, wherever practicable, of the system of task-work, accompanied of course with a law for securing to the slave his little peculium. He recommended also, though with less confidence, a plan for instituting among the slaves a sort of juries for the trial of petty offences—a measure which, he added, he had heard had been tried successfully in two instances in Jamaica, and which a humane proprietor of Barbadoes, the late Mr. Steele, introduced, and for many years maintained with great advantage on his own estate. Another measure, which, as he truly stated, was of less doubtful efficacy, was strongly enforced by him ; namely, the duty of rendering the Sabbath a day of rest and religious improvement, by suppressing the Sunday markets, which he justly declared to be a disgrace to a Christian country. But above all the rest, he pressed the reform of what he represented the greatest of all the Negro's grievances, and which he afterwards brought to the notice of the British Parliament. This was the liability of the slaves to be sold by creditors, under executions for the payment of debts. This grievance he alleged to be upheld and confirmed, though not originally created, by a British Act of Parliament, 5 Geo. II. cap. 7., which, he contended, it was necessary to repeal, in order to enable the colonial legislatures to do away with the practice altogether. He declared it to be a grievance, remorseless and tyrannical in its principle, and dreadful in its effects ; a grievance too which it could not be urged occurred but seldom. "Unhappily," he added, "it occurs every day, and, under the present system, will continue to occur, so long as men shall continue to be unfortunate. Let this statute then," said he, "be totally repealed. Let the Negroes be attached to the land, and sold with it." He even arraigned the Abolitionists as eminently criminal for not having solicited the repeal of that "execrable statute." as he termed it, though of its operation and even existence, nineteen-twentieths of them perhaps were utterly ignorant. With no little pomp and circumstance did this gentleman introduce and carry through Parliament, an act for repealing the statute complained of; and he had the cordial and unanimous support of all the Abolitionists. This measure seemed to pledge the Assemblies in the most effectual manner to follow up the principle of the repealing act, by repealing also their own laws which supported, and had in fact first introduced, the cruel practice: and this experiment on their humanity was tried, it must be admitted, under the most favourable circumstances; for Mr. B. Edwards's proposal of attaching the slaves to the land was strongly recommended to their adoption by the Duke of Portland, then secretary of state for the colonies, a nobleman well known to be peculiarly acceptable to them, in a circular letter to the Governors. Yet of all our colonial legislatures, then thirteeen in number, not one has in any degree reformed the grievance in question, much less followed the suggestion of Mr. Edwards, by attaching the slaves to the plantations. The House of Assembly of Jamaica contemptuously declined giving any answer at all to the Governor's message upon the subject; and the slaves are still every where subject to that " *remorseless and tyrannical grievance*," which above three-and-twenty years ago was so feelingly denounced to, and condemned by, the British Parliament.

Other mitigations of slavery have as long been recommended to the Assemblies, even by their own most respected advocates in this country; but not one has been effectually adopted. The laws which the various legislatures have passed for such purposes, still precisely answer the description given by Mr. Burke, in his letter to Mr. Secretary Dundas, in 1792, of such colonial statutes : " I have seen," said he, after the passing of the celebrated consolidated Slave Laws of Jamaica, and of other islands, " I have seen what has been done by the West-Indian Assemblies. It is arrant trifling;—they have done little, and what they have done is *good for nothing, for it is totally destitute of an executory principle.*" Taking into consideration all the circumstances that accompanied and followed the enactment of those laws, it is difficult to suppose that they were not passed on the views stated in the memorable letter before noticed of the Governor of Dominica, and which indeed seem to have been virtually recommended to them in 1797 by the West-Indian Committee; as the objects suggested to them by that body were " the joint purposes of opposing the plan of the

Abolitionists *," (*i. e.* the abolition of the Slave Trade,)
" and establishing the character of the West-Indian body."
One grand class of such laws, passed indeed at a considerably later period,—the acts of the colonial assemblies
for registering the slaves, with a view to prevent illicit importation,—are shewn, by a Report of the African Institution, to be wholly and manifestly ineffectual to their purpose. But the case, in several of the islands, is still more
opprobrious ; new laws have been passed, which so far
from even exhibiting any show of a wish to alleviate the
pressure of the yoke of slavery, have rendered it more
dreadfully galling, and less tolerable, because even more
than before hopeless. The individual manumission of
slaves by their masters, which has been provided for, with
so much sound policy as well as true humanity, by the laws
in force in the Spanish colonies, and has there been found
productive of such happy effects ; those individual manumissions which, while slavery prevailed here, the English
law assiduously encouraged and promoted, have been
cruelly restrained. They were long since, in one or two
of our islands, subjected to discouraging regulations ; but
were, in most of our colonies, wholly unrestrained till within
the last thirty years. Can it be conceived possible, that
even since the mitigation of slavery was recommended
from the throne, in consequence of addresses from Parliament, several of the colonial legislatures have for the
first time imposed, and others have greatly augmented, the
fines to be paid into their treasuries on the enfranchising
of slaves, so that in some colonies they amount nearly to
an entire pohibition? Such acts may be truly said to be
more unjust in their principle, and more cruel and dangerous in their effects, than almost any other part of the
dreadful code of West-Indian legislation. The laws of
England, ever favourable to manumissions, progressively
rooted out the curse of slavery from our native land ; but

* It is, in the original, " the plan of Mr. Wilberforce." See papers of
1804. St. Vincent's, I. 7.

it is the opposite and opprobrious tendency of these colonial laws to make the barbarous institution perpetual.

I press these topics the more earnestly, because there has prevailed among many of our statesmen, of late years, a most unwarrantable and pernicious disposition to leave all that concerns the well-being of the slaves to the colonial legislatures. Surely this is a course manifestly contrary to the clearest obligations of duty. The very relation in which the Negro slaves and the members of the colonial assemblies, which consist wholly of their masters, stand towards each other, is of itself a decisive reason why the imperial Legislature ought to consider itself bound to exercise the office of an umpire, or rather of a judge between them, as constituting two parties of conflicting interests and feelings. •And this, let it be remembered, not merely because, knowing the frailty of our common nature, and its disposition to abuse absolute power, we ought not to deliver the weaker party altogether into the power of the stronger ; but because in the present instance there are peculiar objections of great force, some of which have been already noticed. In truth, West Indians must be exempt from the ordinary frailties of human nature, if, living continually with those wretched beings, and witnessing their extreme degradation and consequent depravity, they could entertain for the Negroes, in an unimpaired degree, that equitable consideration and that fellow-feeling, which are due from man to man ; so as to sympathise properly with them in their sufferings and wrongs, or form a just estimate of their claims to personal rights and moral improvement.

The fact is, that though the old prejudice, that the Negroes are creatures of an inferior nature, is no longer maintained in terms, there is yet too much reason to fear that a latent impression arising from it still continues practically to operate in the colonies, and to influence the minds of those who have the government of the slaves, in estimating their physical claims, and still more those of their moral nature. The Colonists, indeed, and the Abolitionists would differ as to facts, in speaking of the sufficiency of the slave's supply of food, and of his treatment in some other particulars. But on what other principle than that of the inferiority of the species, can it be explained, that, in estimating what is due to the Negroes, all consideration of their moral nature has been altogether left out? When it is undeniable that they have no more power of giving their testimony against any White ruffian by whom they may have been maltreated, than if they were of the brute creation; that they are worked like cattle under the whip; that they are strangers to the institution of marriage, and to all the blessed truths of Christianity; how, but from their supposed inferiority of nature, could we nevertheless be assured by the colonial legislatures, with the most unhesitating confidence, that whatever defects there might formerly have been in their treatment, they are now as well used *as can reasonably be desired?* If such be indeed their opinion, whether that opinion proceeds from the views here intimated or not, it would still suffice to show the criminality, of our committing to them the destiny of the slaves. For let it be observed, there is not in this instance any difference as to the facts of the case; nor do the colonists affirm what we deny, as to the moral degradation of the slaves. Both parties, for instance, agree that promiscuous intercourse between the sexes, and Pagan darkness, are nearly universal among them; and yet the colonists contend that the slaves are as well treated and governed as they need to be. Can then the members of the British Parliament conscientiously devolve the duty of establishing such religious and moral reforms, as I trust it must be the universal wish of every member of the empire to introduce among the Negroes, upon those, who, to say nothing of the extremity of personal degradation, consider marriage and Christianity as unworthy of their regard, in estimating the condition of their fellow-creatures?

Indeed, the West Indians, in the warmth of argument, have gone still farther, and have even distinctly told us, again and again,—and I am shocked to say that some of their partizans in this country have re-echoed the assertion,—that

these poor degraded beings, the Negro slaves, are as well
or even better off than our British peasantry; a proposition so monstrous, that nothing can possibly exhibit in a
stronger light the extreme force of the prejudices which
must exist in the minds of its assertors. A Briton to
compare the state of a West-Indian slave with that of an
English freeman, and to give the former the preference!
It is to imply an utter insensibility of the native feelings
and moral dignity of man, no less than of the rights of
Englishmen!! I will not condescend to argue this question,
as I might, on the ground of comparative feeding and
clothing, and lodging, and medical attendance. Are these
the only claims ; are these the chief privileges of a rational
and immortal being? Is the consciousness of personal
independence nothing? Are self-possession and self-government nothing? Is it of no account that our persons are
inviolate by any private authority, and that the whip is
placed only in the hands of the public executioner? Is it
of no value that we have the power of pursuing the occu-
pation and the habits of life which we prefer ; that we have
the prospect, or at least the hope, of improving our condition, and of rising, as we have seen others rise, from
poverty and obscurity to comfort, and opulence, and
distinction? Again ; are all the charities of the heart,
which arise out of the domestic relations, to be considered
as nothing ; and, I may add, all their security too among
men who are free agents, and not vendible chattels, liable
continually to be torn from their dearest connections, and
sent into a perpetual exile? Are husband and wife, parent
and child, terms of no meaning? Are willing services, or
grateful returns for voluntary kindnesses, nothing? But,
above all, is Christianity so little esteemed among us, that
we are to account as of no value the "hope full of immortality," the light of heavenly truth, and all the consolations
and supports by which religion cheers the hearts, and ele-
vates the principles, and dignifies the conduct of multitudes
of our labouring classes in this free and enlightened country? Is it nothing to be taught that all human distinctions

will soon be at an end ; that all the labours and sorrows of poverty and hardship will soon exist no more ; and to know, on the express authority of Scripture, that the lower classes, instead of being an inferior order in the creation, are even the preferable objects of the love of the Almighty ?

But such wretched sophisms as insult the understandings of mankind, are sometimes best answered by an appeal to their feelings. Let me therefore ask, is there, in the whole of the three kingdoms, a parent or a husband so sordid and insensible that any sum, which the richest West-Indian proprietor could offer him, would be deemed a compensation for his suffering his wife or his daughter to be subjected to the brutal outrage of the cart-whip— to the savage lust of the driver—to the indecent, and degrading, and merciless punishment of a West-Indian whipping? If there were one so dead, I say not to every liberal, but to every natural feeling, as that money could purchase of him such concessions, such a wretch, and he alone, would be capable of the farther sacrifices necessary for degrading an English peasant to the condition of a West-Indian slave. He might consent to sell the liberty of his own children, and to barter away even the blessings conferred on himself by that religion which declares to him that his master, no less than himself, has a Master in heaven—a common Creator, who is no respecter of persons and in whose presence he may weekly stand on the same spiritual level with his superiors in rank, to be reminded of their common origin, common responsibility, and common day of final and irreversible account.

But I will push no farther a comparison which it is painful and humiliating to contemplate : let it however be remembered, that it is to those who have professed insensibility to this odious contrast that the destiny of the poor slaves would be committed, were we to leave them to the disposal of the colonial legislatures.

There is another consideration, which, on a moment's reflection, will appear perhaps not less decisive. The ad-

vocates for the Negroes declare without reserve, as from
the first they declared, that the reforms they wish to introduce are intended, by preparing the slaves for the possession
of self-government, for the purpose of gradually and safely
doing away slavery altogether, and transmuting the wretched Africans into the condition of free British labourers.
Now, let it never be forgotten, the West-Indian legislatures, and almost all the colonists, with one concurrent
voice, declare that the emancipation of the slaves, within
any period except that to which an antediluvian might
have looked forward, would be their utter ruin. Shall we
then devolve the duty of introducing into the West-Indian
system, the moral reforms which, once effected, would
render it manifestly impossible to detain the slave in his
present degrading bondage, on those who plainly tell us
that his being delivered from it would be productive of their
utter ruin? Can they be expected to labour fairly in producing reforms, the ultimate object of which they do not
merely regard as superfluous, but dread as most pernicious
and destructive? Should we act thus in any parallel instance? All comparisons on this subject are weak; but
suppose that, through a criminal inadvertency, we had
administered some poisonous substance to a fellow-
creature, who had a special claim to our protection and
kindness, that we had deeply injured his constitution,
and that the comfort of all his future life, or probably
his life itself, should depend on his being immediately put
under a course of the ablest medical treatment. Supposing
also—surely,in such a case, no unnatural supposition—that
we felt the deepest distress of mind from the consciousness
of the wrong we had done to this poor sufferer, and were
prompted, alike by conscience and feeling, to use our
utmost possible endeavours to restore him to ease and
health,—should we be satisfied with committing this patient
into the hands of some medical practitioner, whom otherwise we might have been disposed to employ, if he were to
state to us, contrary to our plain knowledge of the fact,
"The man has taken no poison—his health has sustained

no injury—he is already as sound and well as he needs to be, and requires no farther medical care." But we may put the case still more strongly;—Supposing there were a declared opposition of interest between the patient and the same medical practitioner, and that the latter conceived that the recovery of the patient would prove fatal to his own future fortunes,—could we then, as honest and rational men, commit the case to his uncontrouled management alone? If we did, who would not pronounce our alleged sorrow for the injury we had done, and our earnest wish to repair it, to be no better than hypocritical affectation?

Let me not be conceived to dwell on this topic with unreasonable pertinacity. In truth, practically speaking, the fate of the Negro Slaves, so far at least as a safe and peaceable reform of the system is in question, hinges entirely on this point. Of this the colonists themselves are well aware: and, wise in their generation, they therefore take their principal stand on the ground of objecting to the interference of the imperial legislature, for the protection of the slaves ;—though this is an objection which did not even so much as present itself to the inquiring mind of Mr. Burke, when, in the year 1780, he drew up his plan for the reformation of the Negro system ; or in 1792, when he communicated it to his Majesty's Ministers. For we cannot suppose that had it suggested itself to his mind, as an obstacle to the introduction of his plan, he would have left it quite unnoticed. Few, if any, are bold enough to claim for the assemblies an exclusive juris-diction on these subjects as their right. They only tell us of the delicacy of parliamentary interference in such matters of internal legislation. This delicacy, however, was not felt, I repeat it, by Mr. Burke. As little was it felt by Mr. Dundas, the avowed advocate of the Colonies, when, in 1792, he brought forward his plan of emancipa-tion. We may therefore certainly conclude, that no such objection occurred to that experienced statesman, who, as a Minister of the Crown, was called on for great circum-spection, especially in regard to measures proposed by himself, but who, like Mr. Burke, never condescended to notice any such objection to the plan which he laid before the House of Commons.

To persons not conversant with the state of things in the West Indies, it may appear plausible to say, that the assemblies and their constituents are the most competent, in point of information, to the important work of reform and many are apt, perhaps, to be misled by a supposed analogy between the relations of master and slave in the West Indies, and those of the owner or occupier of land and his labourers in this country. But there is in fact no just analogy between them, nor are the colonial legislatures composed of such men as the West-Indian proprietors whom we are accustomed to see in this country; many of whom are personally strangers to their estates, and to the crimes and miseries of the system by which they are governed. Nor is the moral state of the Whites resident in the West Indies, less different from that of the corresponding classes of our countrymen in their native land. It has been most truly remarked by Mr. Brougham, in his able work on Colonial Policy, that the agriculture of the West Indies has always been of a nature nearly allied to commercial adventure; and the spirit of adventure, as he justly observes, is, in such circumstances, unfavourable to morals and to manners. Mr. B. means of course, as the context shews, not such commercial enterprise as belongs to the mercantile character in its proper element, but that of which man is the subject, in the gaming agricultural speculations of a sugar colony. He means, that it gives none of the proper virtues of the industrious European merchant, and still less of those steady local attachments which belong to the landed proprietor here, and make him the natural patron of the labouring class, settled on his hereditary property. "The object of a West-India resident speculator," he observes, " is not to live, but to gain; not to enjoy, but to save; not to subsist in the colonies, but to prepare for shining in the mother country." This I am well aware will be an offensive, as I am sure it is to me a

painful, topic ; but it ought not on that account to be left
out of view : and any one who wishes to form a just notion
of the effects of these causes will find them stated in the
work above-mentioned, with the accustomed force of that
very powerful writer*. Even in the French islands, where
there have been always far more resident proprietors
than in our own, the same causes are stated by Mr. Ma-
louet, himself a colonist, to operate powerfully, and to produce in a considerable degree similar bad effects.

And is it to societies consisting of such elements as these,
that a humane and enlightened legislature can conscientiously delegate its duties as to religious and moral reforms ; reforms too, as has been already shewn, which the
colonists not only slight as frivolous, but condemn as ruinous ? Let it be farther taken into account, that the forma-
tion of laws and regulations for the slaves is not left to the
uncontrouled sentiments and feelings of the more affluent,
and consequently, it may be presumed, more liberal of the

* Mr. Brougham must be understood to intend to state only the tendency and general effects of the causes he has been enumerating.
When individuals manifest that they are exceptions to the rule, it is so
much the more to their honour. " A colony," he remarks, " composed
of such adventurers, is peopled by a race of men all hastening to grow
rich, and eager to acquire wealth for the gratification of avarice, or
voluptuousness." " The continuance of the members in this society is
as short as possible." " What," they may be supposed to say to themselves, " what, though our conduct is incorrect, and our manners dissolute ? we shall accommodate them to those of our European countrymen when we return." " Such, I fear, is the natural language of men in
those circumstances. But their manners are affected also by other
peculiarities in their situation. The want of modest female society,
the general case on the plantations remote from the towns, while it
brutalizes the mind and manners of men, necessarily deprives them of
all the virtuous pleasures of domestic life, and frees them from those
restraints which the presence of a family always imposes on the conduct of the most profligate men. The witnesses of the planter's actions
are the companions of his debaucheries, or the wretched beings who
tremble at his nod, while they minister to the indulgence of his brutal
appetite; and impose no more check upon his excesses, than if they
wanted that faculty of speech which almost alone distinguishes them
from the beasts that surround them."

resident land-owners. For the colonial house of assembly,
which answers to our house of commons, is chosen by the
resident White proprietors at large, and must necessarily
be governed in great measure by their general sentiments
and feelings. Nor can it be supposed to be uninfluenced
by what is here called the popular voice, but which, in the
West Indies, is the voice of the White colonists only,
and these too of the lower order, among whom the *esprit de
corps* is peculiarly strong. These borderers on the despised coloured race are naturally the most hostile to them,
and the most tenacious of those complexional privileges
which constitute their own social elevation. The voice,
therefore, of the populace in the West Indies, or what may
be called the cry of the mob, is always adverse to the humane and liberal principles by which the slavery of the
Blacks should be mitigated, and by which they should be
gradually prepared for the enjoyment of freedom.

These considerations are of no trifling moment; and
they may be, in some measure, illustrated by some transactions which took place not long ago in the largest, except Jamaica, and the longest settled of all our colonies,
the island of Barbadoes ; though there are in that colony
more resident proprietors than in any other, in proportion
to the whole population. The facts I here allude to may
have the more weight, because they are not liable to the
objection, which has been sometimes urged against the
Abolitionists when they have quoted laws and transactions
of an old date, that they formed an unfair test of the opinions and feelings of the present generation ; for they took
place so recently as the latter part of 1804.

It had long been a reproach to Barbadoes, that the
murder of a slave by his owner, instead of being a capital
crime, as in most of our other West-Indian colonies, was,
in that colony, punishable only by a fine of 15*l.** Lord

* The murder of another man's slave was punished more severely,
the penalty being then 25*l.* to be paid to the public treasury, and double
the slave's value to the owner. But to subject the criminal to any

Seaforth, the governor, therefore, himself a West-Indian proprietor, wishing to wipe off the blot, sent a message, in the common form, to the house of assembly, recommending that an act should be passed to make the murder of a slave a capital felony. There seems every reason to believe that the council, or colonial house of lords, would gladly have assented to the proposition. But, strange as it may appear to those who are unacquainted with West-Indian prejudices, notwithstanding the time and manner in which the proposition was brought forward, the house of assembly absolutely refused to make the alteration.

If the bare statement of this fact must shock every liberal mind, how much will the shock be increased, when it is known under what circumstances it was that this refusal took place! For it had happened very recently, that several most wanton and atrocious murders had been committed on slaves; and some of them accompanied with circumstances of the most horrid and disgusting barbarity. Lord Seaforth felt all the horror likely to be produced by such incidents in a generous and feeling mind. He writes thus to Lord Camden, then the Secretary of State for the Colonies:—" I inclose the Attorney-general's letter to me on the subject of the Negroes so most wantonly murdered. I am sorry to say, *several other instances of the same barbarity* have occurred, with which I have not troubled your Lordship, as I only wished to make you acquainted with the subject in general." It is due to Mr. Beccles, the Attorney-general, and to Mr. Coulthurst, the Advocate-general, to state, that they also felt and expressed themselves on the occasion just as persons in the same rank of life would have done in this country. Lord Sea-

punishment, the murder was to have been committed " of wantonness, or only of bloody mindedness, or cruel intention; and lest there should be any disposition to visit the crime too severely, it was specially enacted, that " if any Negro or other slave under punishment by his master or his order, for running away, *or any other crimes or misdemeanours towards his said master, unfortunately shall suffer in life or member, which seldom happens, no persons whatsoever shall be liable to any fine therefore," forth also thus described the official papers he transmitted as to the murders he had mentioned in some former letters : " They are selected from *a great number,* among which there is not one in contradiction of the horrible facts. The truth is, that nothing has given me more trouble to get to the bottom of, than this business, *so horribly absurd are the prejudices of the people.* However, a great part of my object is answered by the alarm my interference has excited, and the attention it has called to the business. Bills are already proposed to make murder felony in both the council and the assembly ; but I fear they will be thrown out for the present in the assembly : the council are unanimous on the side of humanity *." Lord Seaforth's predic-

---

* The letter from the Attorney-general of Barbadoes to Lord Seaforth throws so much light on the popular feeling of the lower class of White men in Barbadoes, that it ought not to be suppressed, although it is a humiliating and disgusting recital :—" Extract of a letter from the Attorney-general of Barbadoes to the Governor of the Island :-
' A Mr. ———, the manager of a plantation in the neighbourhood, had some months before purchased an African lad, who was much attached to his person, and slept in a passage contiguous to his chamber. On Sunday night there was an alarm of fire in the plantation, which induced Mr. ——— to go out hastily, and the next morning he missed the lad, who he supposed intended to follow him in the night, and had mistaken his way. He sent to his neighbours, and to Mr. C. among the rest, to inform them that his African lad had accidentally strayed from him ; that he could not speak a word of English, and that possibly he might be found breaking canes, or taking something else for his support ; in which case, he requested that they would not injure him, but return him, and he, Mr. ——— himself, would pay any damage he might have committed. A day or two after, the owner of the boy was informed, that Mr. C. and H. had killed a Negro in a neighbouring gully, and buried him there. He went to Mr. C. to inquire into the truth of the report, and intended to have the grave opened, to see whether it was his African lad. *Mr. C. told him a Negro had been killed and buried there ; but assured him it was not his, for he knew him very well, and he need not be at the trouble of opening the grave. Upon this the owner went away satisfied.* But receiving further information, which left no doubt upon his mind that it was his Negro, he returned, and opened the grave, and found it to be so. I was his leading counsel, and the facts stated in my brief were as follows : That C. and H. being informed that there was a Negro lurking in the gully, went armed with muskets, and took several Negro men with them. The poor African, seeing a parcel of men coming to

tion was but too fully verified;—the assembly threw out the bill, and the law against wilful murder remained in its pristine state.

attack him, was frightened: he took up a stone to defend himself, and retreated into a cleft rock, where they could not easily come at him : they then went for some trash, put it into the crevices of the rock behind him, and set it on fire : after it had burnt so as to scorch the poor fellow, he ran into a pool of water close by : they sent a Negro to bring him out, and he threw the stone at the Negro ; upon which the two White men fired several times at him with the guns loaded with shot, and the Negroes pelted him with stones. He was at length dragged out of the pool in a dying condition ; for he had not only received several bruises from the stones, but his breast was so pierced with the shot, that it was like a cullender. *The White savages ordered the Negroes to dig a grave ; and whilst they were digging it, the poor creature made signs of begging for water, which was not given to him, but, as soon as the grave was dug, he was thrown into it and covered over ; and there seems to be some doubt whether he was then quite dead.* C. and H. deny this ; but the owner assured me that he could prove it by more than one witness ; and I have reason to believe it to be true, because on the day of trial C. and H. did not suffer the cause to come to a hearing, but paid the penalties and the costs of suit, which it is not supposed they would have done had they been innocent.

"I have the honour to be, &c."

The same transaction, with another far more dreadful murder, in which there was a deliberate ingenuity of cruelty which almost exceeds belief, but of which I will spare my readers the recital, is related, with scarcely any variation as to circumstances, by the Advocate-general, who, as well as the gentleman of whose estate the criminal was the manager, and who was at the time absent, expressed their most lively indignation against such horrid cruelty. It may be proper to remark, that the story of the poor boy strikingly shews that such protection as the Negro slave occasionally receives from the laws, is too often to be ascribed rather to the master's care of his property, than to any more generous motive. The master, in this case, when he had only reason to believe that a Negro had been killed and buried out of the way, and not that it was his own slave, goes away satisfied. Is there a human being who in this country would have so done ? Again, it is a suggestion which the circumstances of the story enforce on us, that the crowd which was now collected, instead of being shocked at such barbarity, were rather abettors of it ; and then we hear the White savages (as the Attorney-general justly styles them) order the Negroes who were present to dig a grave for their wretched countryman. They knew their state too well to refuse ; and accordingly, with a promptitude of obedience which, with all our ideas of their sunk and prostrate spirits, must surprise us, they immediately executed the order.

I should be glad to be able to refer the conduct of the assembly, in this instance, altogether to the influence of the lower orders over their minds. This, doubtless, we may hope, had some share in producing the effect; though, considering that in their circumstances it was peculiarly their duty to set the tone of public judgment and feeling to the bulk of the community, this would not be a very creditable plea. But it is due to truth to remark, that there is no hint to this effect in the papers laid before the House of Commons: on the contrary, in the Assembly's answer, there is an expression of resentment against the Governor, and an intimation of the danger of interfering between master and slave.

This incident will exhibit to every considerate reader a striking specimen of the state of the public mind in the West Indies, at least so recently as 1805, in regard to the African race : and it may serve in some degree to shew the error into which we should fall, by conceiving that the bulk of the White population in our colonies, in estimating the proper conduct to be observed towards the slaves, would think and feel like ourselves. Even in this land of liberty and humanity, acts of atrocious cruelty have been perpetrated. We have heard of an apprentice being starved to death by her mistress ; and, more recently, the British Governor of an African settlement caused the death of a soldier by excessive punishment. But what was the effect on the public mind ? In both cases, it was difficult to prevent the populace from anticipating the execution of the sentence of the law. In Barbadoes, on the contrary, the proposal to punish such enormities by more than a small fine, was just as unpopular as it would be in this country, to inflict a punishment which should be utterly disproportionate to the crime—such as hanging a man for petty larceny. Except among the highest and best educated classes, the natural sympathy was reversed ; and the most horrible murders, some of them attended with circumstances too shocking for recital, instead of exciting any just commiseration for the Negro race, had actually worked in the opposite direction. And is it to assemblies subject to the influence of such popular prejudices as these, and sitting in the bosom of such communities, that we can commit the temporal and eternal interests of many hundred thousands of these despised fellow-creatures?

If this case itself suggests to us a useful distrust of the colonial assemblies, in what relates to the Negroes, the sequel of it will not perhaps be less useful in enabling us to judge of their probable conduct, even when they may profess a disposition to conform to our wishes. Whether it was that the influence of the higher members of the Barbadoes community worked at last upon the minds of the Assembly, or that the effect likely to be produced in the English Parliament led to a change of conduct, so it was that the Assembly ultimately gave way; and it was supposed, that by the new law of Barbadoes, no less than by that of the other islands, the wilful murder of a slave was made a capital offence. Such, indeed, was the statement made afterwards by more than one advocate for the West Indians, in the controversy in 1816, concerning the Registry Bill; and the Abolitionists were reproached with having referred to a period when the law had been different, as if it had been of an antiquated date. Yet, when the statute book itself was examined, (which, I confess, not doubting the accuracy of the statement, I did not look into for several years), it was found that the alleged reformation of the law is highly problematical at least, if not clearly and totally evasive; for, instead of simply declaring the well-defined crime of wilful murder to be a capital felony when perpetrated on a slave, the enacting words are; " If any person shall hereafter wilfully, *maliciously*, *wantonly*, and WITHOUT PROVOCATION, kill and murder any slave, &c." If, hereafter, any of those " *White Savages*," so justly termed such by the Attorney-general of Barbadoes, in wreaking their vengeance on the wretched subjects of their tyranny, should actually murder any of their slaves, or the slaves of others, would there be a hope, even if all the scarcely superable obstacles arising from the absolute rejection of Negro testimony were to be overcome, of a conviction under the terms of this act? What offender could be unable to prove, to the satisfaction of a Barbadoes jury, that there had been *some provocation?* Yet this is the amended, the ameliorating law passed in April, 1805, entitled, "An Act for the *better Protection* of the Slaves of this Island *."

Surely, with these and the many other evidences we have had of the state of mind respecting Negroes, which prevails in the Colonies, we should be more culpable than they, if we were still to commit implicitly to their legislatures the task of devising and carrying into execution such physical and moral reforms as humanity demands in the slavery of the West Indies. More culpable, I say it advisedly; for, though it is no praise to us, but to the good providence of God, we are exempt from the influence of the harsh prejudices to which they, in some degree by our concurrent fault, have been subjected.

The information also which we now possess, as to the African character, would aggravate our criminality. For though the day, I trust, is gone by for ever, in which the alleged inferiority of intellect and incurable barbarity of the African race were supposed to extenuate their oppression, yet it ought not to be left unnoticed, that the notions which formerly prevailed to their prejudice, in these respects, have of late years been abundantly refuted, not only by authority but experience. It may be confidently affirmed, that there never was any uncivilized people of whose dispositions we have received a more amiable character than that which is given of the Native Africans by Parke and Golberry, both of whom visited those districts of Africa from which victims for the Slave Trade were furnished;

---

* See papers entitled Colonial Laws respecting Slaves, 1788—1815 ordered by the House of Commons to be printed, 5th April, 1816.

and whose testimony in their favour will naturally be admitted with less reserve, because neither of them could be
biassed by any wish to discountenance the Slave Trade,
they having evidently felt no desire for its abolition.

But it is at Sierra Leone, that long despised and calum-
niated colony, that the African character has been most
effectually and experimentally vindicated. The first seeds
of civilization which were sown there by the Christian
philanthropy of Mr. Granville Sharpe nearly perished from
the unkindly soil to which they had been committed; but
they were saved from early 'destruction, and cultured at
length successfully, under the fostering care and indefa-
tigable attention of the late excellent Mr. H. Thornton,
and by other good and able men, who, both at home and
in the colony, co-operated with him ; by one living bene-
factor especially, who will be hereafter venerated as the
steady, enlightened, and unwearied, though unostentatious
friend of Africa. It is at Sierra Leone that the great experiment on human nature has been tried ; and there it
has appeared, that the poor African barbarians, just
rescued from the holds of slave-ships, are capable, not
merely of being civilized, but of soon enjoying, with advantage, the rights and institutions of British freemen.
In truth, to have formed any conclusions against the
Negroes from the experience we had of them in their state
of bondage, was not less unphilosophical than unjust. It
was remarked by M. Dupuis, the British consul at Moga-
dore, that even the generality of European Christians,
after a long captivity and severe treatment among the
Arabs, appeared at first exceedingly stupid and insensible.
" If," he adds, " they have been any considerable time in
slavery, they appear lost to reason and feeling ; their
spirits broken, and their faculties sunk in a species of
stupor which I am unable adequately to describe. They
appear degraded even below the Negro slave. The succession of hardships, without any protecting law to which
they can appeal for any alleviation or redress, seems to
destroy every spring of exertion or hope in their minds.

They appear indifferent to every thing around them; abject, servile, and brutish *."

If the native intelligence and buoyant independence of Britons cannot survive in the dank and baleful climate of personal slavery, could it be reasonably expected that the poor Africans, unsupported by any consciousness of personal dignity or civil rights, should not yield to the malignant influences to which they had so long been subjected, and be depressed even below the level of the human species? But at Sierra Leone, they have resumed the stature and port of men, and have acquired, in an eminent degree, the virtues of the citizen and the subject. Witness the peace, and order, and loyalty which have generally prevailed in this colony, in a remarkable degree; especially under the present excellent Governor, Sir Charles Mac-Carthy. Still more, these recent savages, having become the subjects of religious and moral culture, have manifested the greatest willingness to receive instruction, and made a practical proficiency in Christianity, such as might put Europeans to the blush. Not only have they learned with facility the principles of the Christian faith, but they have shewn, by their mutual kindnesses, and by the attachment and gratitude to their worthy pastors and superintendents, that they have derived from their knowledge of Christianity its moral and practical fruits.

The same testimony as to the progress of the Negro children, in common school learning, has been given by all the masters who have instructed them in the island of Hayti; and the missionaries, in our different West-Indian islands, testify, with one consent, the gratitude and attachment which the West-Indian, no less than the Sierra Leone Negroes feel to those who condescend to become their teachers.

Again; the impression so assiduously attempted heretofore to be made, that the *indolence* of the Negro race was utterly incurable, and that without the driving whip they

* See Quarterly Review for January 7, 1816.—Article, *Tombuctoo.*

never would willingly engage in agricultural labour, has been shewn to be utterly without foundation. Mr. Parke relates, that the Africans, when prompted by any adequate motives, would work diligently and perseveringly both in agricultural and manufacturing labours. And there is on the African coast a whole nation of the most muscular men and the hardiest labourers, who, from their known industry, are hired both for government service, and by the European traders, as workmen, both on ship-board and on shore.

Nor have instances of a similar kind been wanting even in the West Indies, whenever circumstances have been at all favourable to voluntary industry. Since the dissolution of the Black corps, (a measure which the Abolitionists are scarcely, I fear, excusable for not having opposed, though prompted to acquiesce in it by unwillingness to thwart, when not indispensably necessary, the prejudices of the colonists,) many of the disbanded soldiers have maintained themselves by their own agricultural labours, and have manifested a degree of industry that ought to have silenced for ever all imputations on the diligence of their race. But another still more striking instance has been lately afforded in Trinidad. There many hundreds of American Negroes, at the close of the late unhappy war with the United States, were, by the humane policy of Sir Ralph Woodford, received into Trinidad, to the no small alarm of the planters. These were slaves enfranchised by desertion; yet, instead of becoming a nuisance to the community by idleness and dissolute manners, as prejudice loudly foretold, they have maintained themselves well, in various ways, by their own industry and prudence. Many of them have worked as hired labourers for the planters with so much diligence and good conduct, that they are now universally regarded as a valuable acquisition to the colony : and it is supposed, that a large addition to their number would be gladly received.

Are all these important lessons to be read to us without producing any influence on our minds? Ought they not to enforce on us, as by a voice from Heaven, that we have been most cruelly and inexcusably degrading, to the level of brutes, those whom the Almighty had made capable of enjoying our own civil blessings in this world, not less clearly than he has fitted them to be heirs of our common immortality?

But while we are loudly called on by justice and humanity to take measures without delay for improving the condition of our West-Indian Slaves, self-interest also inculcates the same duty, and with full as clear a voice. It is a great though common error, that notwithstanding we must, on religious and moral grounds, condemn the West-Indian system, yet that, in a worldly view, it has been eminently gainful both to individuals and to the community at large. On the contrary, I believe it might be proved to any inquiring and unprejudiced mind, that, taking in all considerations of political economy, and looking to the lamentable waste of human life among our soldiers and seamen, raised and recruited at a great expense, as well as to the more direct pecuniary charge of protecting the sugar colonies, no system of civil polity was ever maintained at a greater price, or was less truly profitable either to individuals or to the community, than that of our West-Indian settlements. Indeed, it would have been a strange exception to all those established principles which Divine Providence has ordained for the moral benefit of the world, if national and personal prosperity were generally and permanently to be found to arise from injustice and oppression. There may be individual instances of great fortunes amassed by every species of wrong-doing. A course, ruinous in the long run, may, to an individual, or for a time, appear eminently profitable; nevertheless, it is unquestionably true, that the path of prosperity rarely diverges long and widely from that of integrity and virtue,—or, to express it in a familiar adage, that honesty is the best policy.

It ought not to be necessary to assert such principles as these in an age in which it has been incontrovertibly established by the soundest of our political economists,—that the base and selfish, though plausible views, which formerly prevailed so widely among statesmen, and taught them to believe that the prosperity and elevation of their country would be best promoted by the impoverishment and depression of its neighbours, were quite fallacious; and when we have now learned the opposite and beneficent lesson, —that every nation is, in fact, benefited by the growing affluence of others, and that all are thus interested in the well-being and improvement of all. At such an enlightened period as this, when commerce herself adopts the principles of true morality, and becomes liberal and benevolent, will it be believed that the Almighty has rendered the depression and misery of the cultivators of the soil in our West-Indian colonies necessary, or even conducive, to their prosperity and safety? No, surely! The oppression of these injured fellow-creatures, however it may be profitable in a few instances, can never be generally politic ; and in the main, and ultimately, the comfort of the labourer, and the well-being of those who have to enjoy the fruits of his labour, will be found to be coincident.

As for the apprehensions of ruin, expressed by the West Indians, from the instruction and moral improvement of their slaves, or from the interference of the Imperial Legislature, we have been taught by experience in the Slave-Trade controversy, that their apprehensions are not always reasonable, either in degree, or in the objects to which they are directed. How confidently did all the Slave-traders predict their own ruin, together with that of the West Indies, and also of the town of Liverpool, from the regulations of the bill for limiting the number of slaves to be taken in ships of given dimensions, while the trade should be tolerated, and for requiring certain particulars of food and medical attendance ! yet, after a few years, the regulations were allowed, not merely to be harmless, but to have been positively and greatly beneficial. The total ruin of the sugar colonies was still more confidently foretold by the planters, the assemblies, and their agents, by their parliamentary advocates, and the West-Indian committee, as a sure consequence of abolishing the Slave Trade ; and yet there is not, I believe, an intelligent West-Indian who will not now confess, that it would have been greatly for the benefit of all our old colonies, if the Slave Trade had been abolished many years sooner ; and that, if it had continued some years longer, it must have completed their destruction.

Mr. Dundas, in 1792, did not hesitate to ridicule the vain terrors of the parties whose battle he was fighting, and, by their own selection, as their commander-in-chief, though emancipation itself was the object. In illustration of the apprehensions which many entertained of the consequences of changing their slaves into free labourers, he stated that some years before, in certain districts of Scotland, the persons who laboured in the salt-works and coal-mines were actually slaves ; and that a proposal being made to emancipate them, instantly the owners of the works came forward, declaring that if their vassals were to be raised to the condition of free labourers, they themselves would be utterly ruined,—for that such was the peculiarity, such the unpleasant nature, of those species of labours, that they could not depend on hired service, as in other instances. " But at length," added Mr. Dundas, " the good sense of the age obtained the victory. The salters and colliers were changed into free labourers, and all the terrors of the owners ended in smoke."

While thus alive to imaginary dangers, or rather while thus assiduous in endeavouring to inspire alarm in the mother country, to prevent her listening to the claims of justice and mercy, our planters appear blind to the new and real dangers that are accumulating around them. Providence graciously seems to allow them a golden interval, which, duly improved, might prevent the dreadful explosion that may otherwise be expected. But they neglect it with a supineness and insensibility resembling infatuation. With a community of nearly 800,000 free Blacks, many of them accustomed to the use of arms, within sight of the greatest of our West-Indian islands ; with a slave population in Cuba

and Port Rico, which has been of late so fearfully augmented with imported Africans, as, according to all
received principles, to produce, even in pacific times, and
much more in the present æra of transatlantic convulsions,
the utmost extremity of danger ; with the example afforded in many of the United States, and in almost all the
new Republics of South America, where Negro Slavery
has been recently abolished,—is this a time, are these the
circumstances, in which it can be wise and safe, if it were
even honest and humane, to keep down in their present
state of heathenish and almost brutish degradation, the
800,000 Negroes in our West-Indian colonies? Here,
indeed, is danger, if we observe the signs of the times,
whether we take our lesson from the history of men, or
form our conclusions from natural reason or from the revealed will of God.

But to raise these poor creatures from their depressed
condition, and, if they are not yet fit for the enjoyment of
British freedom, elevate them at least from the level of the
brute creation into that of rational nature—dismiss the
driving whip, and thereby afford place for the development
of the first rudiments of civil character—implant in them
the principle of hope—let free scope be given for their
industry, and for their rising in life by their personal good
conduct—give them an interest in defending the community
to which they belong—teach them that lesson which Christianity can alone truly inculcate, that the present life is but
a short and uncertain span, to which will succeed an eternal
existence of happiness or misery—inculcate on them, on
the authority of the sacred page, that the point of real importance is not what is the rank or the station men occupy, but
how they discharge the duties of life—how they use the
opportunities they may enjoy of providing for their ever-
lasting happiness. Taught by Christianity, they will sustain with patience the sufferings of their actual lot, while
the same instructress will rapidly prepare them for a better ;
and instead of being objects at one time of contempt, and
at another of terror, (a base and servile passion, which too

naturally degenerates into hatred,) they will be soon regarded as a grateful peasantry, the strength of the communities in which they live,—of which they have hitherto been the weakness and the terror, sometimes the mischief and the scourge.

To the real nature of the West-Indian system, and still more to the extent of its manifold abuses, the bulk even of well-informed men in this country are, I believe, generally strangers. May it not be from our having sinned in ignorance that we have so long been spared? But ignorance of a duty which we have had abundant means of knowing to be such, can by no one be deemed excusable. Let us not presume too far on the forbearance of the Almighty. Favoured in an equal degree with Christian light, with civil freedom, and with a greater measure of national blessings than perhaps any other country upon earth ever before enjoyed, what a return would it be for the goodness of the Almighty, if we were to continue to keep the descendants of the Africans, whom we have ourselves wrongfully planted in the western hemisphere, in their present state of unexampled darkness and degradation!

While efforts are making to rescue our country from this guilt and this reproach, let every one remember that he is answerable for any measure of assistance which Providence has enabled him to render towards the accomplishment of the good work. In a country in which the popular voice has a powerful and constitutional influence on the government and legislation, to be silent when there is a question of reforming abuses repugnant to justice and humanity is to share their guilt. Power always implies responsibility; and the possessor of it cannot innocently be neutral, when by his exertion moral good may be promoted, or evil lessened or removed.

If I may presume to employ a few words on what belongs more particularly to the writer of these lines, I can truly declare, that an irresistible conviction that it is his positive duty to endeavour to rouse his countrymen to a just sense of the importance and urgency of our duties

towards the Negro Slaves, has alone compelled him re-
luctantly thus to come forward again in such an arduous
cause as this, and at a period of life when nature shrinks
from a laborious contest. He can but too surely anticipate
from experience, that the grossest and most unfounded
calumnies will be profusely poured out against him ; but he
nevertheless proceeds, animated by the wish, and, he will
add, the confident hope, that the cause of our African
brethren will deeply interest the public mind, and that the
legislature will be induced to adopt the course prescribed
to us by the strongest obligations of moral and religious
duty.

Before I conclude, may I presume to interpose a word
of caution to my fellow-labourers in this great cause,—a
caution which I can truly say I have ever wished myself to
keep in remembrance, and observe in practice : it is, that
while we expose and condemn the evils of the system itself,
we should treat with candour and tenderness the characters
of the West-Indian proprietors. Let not the friends of
the Africans forget that they themselves might have in-
herited West-Indian property ; and that, by early example
and habit, they might have been subjected to the very prejudices which they now condemn. I have before declared,
and I now willingly repeat, that I sincerely believe many
of the owners of West-Indian estates to be men of more
than common kindness and liberality ; but I myself have
found many of them, as I have had every reason to believe,
utterly unacquainted with the true nature and practical
character of the system with which they have the misfortune to be connected.

While, however, we speak and act towards the colonists
personally with fair consideration and becoming candour,
let our exertions in the cause of the unfortunate slaves be
zealous and unremitting. Let us act with energy suited
to the importance of the interests for which we contend.
Justice, humanity, and sound policy prescribe our course,
and will animate our efforts. Stimulated by a consciousness

of what we owe to the laws of God and the rights and happiness of man, our exertions will be ardent, and our perseverance invincible. Our ultimate success is sure; and ere long we shall rejoice in the consciousness of having delivered our country from the greatest of her crimes, and rescued her character from the deepest stain of dishonour.

THE END.

NEGRO SLAVERY;

OR,

A VIEW

OF

SOME OF THE MORE PROMINENT FEATURES

OF

THAT STATE OF SOCIETY,

AS IT EXISTS IN

THE UNITED STATES OF AMERICA

AND IN THE

COLONIES OF THE WEST INDIES,

ESPECIALLY IN

JAMAICA.

CONTENTS.

―――――

NEGRO SLAVERY,

&c. &c.

THE object of the present publication is to furnish to the public a plain, authentic, and unvarnished picture of Negro slavery, not as it may have existed at some antecedent period of time, but as it exists at the present moment, both in the United States of America, and in the European Colonies of the West Indies, which have been peopled by imported Africans. We shall begin with the United States.

THE NEGRO SLAVERY OF THE UNITED STATES.

The real nature of Negro slavery, as it exists in the United States, at the present moment, cannot be better exhibited than by republishing an article which made its appearance not long since in monthly periodical work. It is a review of two volumes of Travels which had recently been published in this country; the one entitled "Travels in Canada and the United States," by Lieut. Francis Hall; and the other, "Sketches of America," by Mr. Fearon. The article is as follows:—

In undertaking the review of the works of Lieutenant Hall and Mr. Fearon, we have no intention to amuse our readers with a description of American scenery, or to communicate information on the politics or statistics of the United States. Neither is it our object to discuss the much-agitated question of the advantages of emigrating to that land of large promise, and, as some allege, of lean performance. We mean to devote the present article to the consideration of a single feature in the picture of American society given by our authors, and on which, as it stands revealed to us in these volumes in all its deformity, we are anxious to fix the regards of our readers. We allude to the NEGRO SLAVERY which pervades a great part of the United States.

The most copious view both of the legal and actual condition of the slave, as it exists in the United States, is to be found in the work of Mr. Hall. It is true, as this intelligent writer observes, that information on their actual state, whether in law or fact, is little attainable by a cursory traveller. The planter, of course, will not present himself for examination, with his memorandum book of the stripes and tortures he has inflicted, and of the groans which have followed. If he affords any information at all on the subject, it passes through a doubly distorted medium. As a planter, he is interested in concealing the evils, and still more the enormities, of Negro servitude ; while, as an American, he is naturally anxious to vindicate the national character in the eyes of a foreigner. Add to this, that the testimony of the slave himself would gain no credit from the enemies to his freedom ; whilst it is almost impossible that the passing traveller, or the occasional guest, should himself witness much of the practical operation of a system, the most odious and frightful part of which is necessarily withdrawn from the public eye. In general, therefore, the traveller has it only in his power to delineate such broad outlines as are incapable of concealment, leaving them to be filled up by means of those fair inductions which, on the admitted principles of human nature, we are authorized to draw from the undisputed facts of the case. And this is all which Mr. Hall or indeed Mr. Fearon, professes to do.

The law by which slaves, and even free Men of Colour, are governed in the Carolinas—and Mr. Hall believes that the same or a similar code prevails in all the *slave* states—is a provincial act passed in 1740, and made perpetual in 1783. It begins with an enactment justly and feelingly stigmatized by our author as a " heart-chilling declaration." It is as follows : " Whereas, in His Majesty's plantations, &c. slavery has been allowed, be it enacted, that all Negroes, Mulattoes, &c. who are or shall hereafter be in this province, and all their issue and offspring, born and to be born, shall

be, and are hereby declared to be, and shall remain for ever hereafter, absolute slaves."

A clause follows, from which Mr. Hall tells us, and we can well
credit his report, that "the most iniquitous oppressions are at this
day deduced." "IT SHALL ALWAYS BE PRESUMED THAT EVERY
NEGRO IS A SLAVE, UNLESS THE CONTRARY CAN BE MADE TO AP-
PEAR *." Hall, p. 422.

The ninth clause gives to two justices of the peace and five free-
holders, who most probably are always slave owners, the power of
trying slaves even for capital offences, and of carrying their sentence
into effect without any reference, which we can discover, to a higher
tribunal; and this court (subject, as it would seem, to no revisal,
and with whose decisions not even the mercy of the governor can in
most cases interfere, no report of its proceedings being made to
him), may inflict such manner of death † "as they shall judge will
be most effectual to deter others from offending in like manner."
Before this tribunal, so formed, the evidence of all free Negroes and
of any slave, is taken against a slave, "without oath ‡."

The thirty-fourth clause forbids any master from suffering a slave
to traffic on his own account §.

The thirty-seventh clause, observes Mr. Hall, presents an exqui-
site specimen of legislative cant and cruelty. It declares "cruelty"
to be "not only highly unbecoming those who profess themselves
Christians, but odious in the eyes of all men who have any sense
of virtue and humanity." It *therefore* enacts, that "to restrain
and prevent barbarity from being exercised towards slaves," "any
person wilfully murdering a slave shall forfeit 700l. currency," that
is 100l. sterling; "and that, if any person shall on a sudden heat

* This appalling principle, we lament to say, is also still the universal rule of law
throughout the whole of our West-Indian possessions. The clumsy attempt which
has recently been made in Jamaica, to modify, by means of a process *de homine replegiando*, its cruel consequences, only serves to establish the opprobrious fact more
incontestibly.

† Fortunately for humanity, the feelings manifested by the British public during
the last thirty years have led to the abolition, in our own colonies, of the cruel modes
of inflicting death which were previously in common use there. Capital punishments
are now confined to hanging.

‡ Such, in general, and with slight and unessential modifications, is also the constitution of the slave courts in our own colonies.

§ In our West Indies, this restriction is for the most part confined to such articles
as form the subjects of the traffic of masters, as sugar, coffee, cotton, cocoa, &c. &c.

and passion, or by undue correction, kill his own slave, or the slave of another person, he shall forfeit 350*l.* currency," or 50*l.* sterling.

The thirty-eighth and thirty-ninth clauses are conceived in a similar spirit. Fourteen pounds (we are not told whether this be currency or sterling, but it matters little,) is the penalty for " cutting out the tongue, dismembering, and other tortures inflicted by any other instrument than a horsewhip, cowskin, or small stick." There is, it is true, a semblance of humanity in the provision which follows, and which enacts, that the master of a slave shall be presumed guilty when his slave is maimed or cruelly beaten; but the whole effect of the clause is destroyed by ordering, that if he should not be able to clear himself of the imputation " by evidence," he may clear himself of it, " BY MAKING OATH TO THE CONTRARY." This is holding out a premium for perjury.

By the forty-third clause, any White man meeting above seven slaves on a high road together, SHALL AND MAY WHIP EACH OF THEM, NOT EXCEEDING TWENTY LASHES ON THE BARE BACK. And by the forty-fifth clause a penalty of 100*l.* currency is inflicted for the crime of teaching a slave to write.

It would be difficult to account for the wanton and superfluous barbarity which is exhibited in these and similar enactments, if we were not to resort, for an explanation of the phenomenon, to the powerful operation, in the breast of masters, of that basest and most cruel of all passions—fear. In this view of the subject, Mr. Hall seems to concur; for he thus closes his account of the slave laws of Carolina :—

" Such is the code by which Christians govern Christians : nor is it, in any point, a dead letter. The fears of the proprietors are tremblingly alive, and racked with the dread of an insurrection, in which they must expect the measure they have meted. A military police is constantly kept up in Charleston ; and every Man of Colour, whether slave or free, found in the streets after dark, without a pass, is taken up and punished*." Hall, p. 424.

But we have scarcely occasion to resort to this principle, in order to account for the practical atrocities of the slave system. The

---

* Mr. Birkbeck, in his " Notes on America," speaks in strong terms of the perpetual state of apprehension in which the planters of Virginia appeared to live, lest their slaves should rise against them.

very existence of absolute slavery on the one hand, and of unre-
stricted power on the other, implies them.

"He," observes Mr. Hall afterwards, "must be a very sanguine
enthusiast in favour of human nature, who believes that the Negro,
thus protected by the laws, will be very tenderly cherished by his
master*. The uncontrolled will of the most virtuous individual
would be a fearful thing to live under; but the brutal passions of
the sordid, the cruel, and the ignorant, scourges which might well
' appal the guilty and confound the free,' are the rule by which at
least nine-tenths of the slave population are governed. If, so governed, they are mildly and justly governed, we must admit the
constant operation in their favour of a miracle strong enough to
invert the whole moral order of nature. To render tigers granivo-
rous would be comparatively easy.

" It is not impossible, but that the house servants and personal
domestics of humane and enlightened masters may be in a condition
not in every respect much worse than that of persons filling the
same station in European countries; but it is not from the good
fortune of this minute portion we can deduce a fair estimate of the
condition of the many. It is on the plantations, and principally,
perhaps, among the petty proprietors, the work of torture goes on.
An occasional instance of atrocity sometimes meets the public eye,
and sheds a lurid light upon a region ' where hope never comes.'"
Hall, pp. 426, 427.

Mr. Hall then states some particulars in the mode of treating
slaves, which he asserts to be matters of public notoriety, admitting
of no dispute, and therefore affording an undeniable foundation on
which to discuss the question of their physical enjoyments. Their
huts are miserable in the last degree, built of unsquared trunks of
pine trees, so ill put together that, during the night, the fire shines
through them as through wire lanterns. And he states it as no
slight addition to their toil to be obliged to cut and fetch wood to
warm this miserable dwelling, pervious as it is to every blast, and
to have their night's rest perpetually broken by the necessity of
keeping up fires to temper the cold†. The furniture of these huts

---

* "The Abolitionists are charged with an affectation of philanthropy, because
they think Black men have the same feelings with White; but it is the very sobriety
of reason, to ascribe to planters the virtues of angels."

† Slaves in the West Indies will, of course, suffer less from cold than those in
America.

consists of a few gourds and wooden utensils, and as for bedding, a Negro is supposed to require none. The accommodation to which even the master who is reputed humane and equitable considers his slaves to be entitled is this wretched cabin with a single blanket. The usual clothing of the plantation slaves, Mr. Hall observed " almost invariably to be ragged and miserable in the extreme." Their food consists of rice and Indian meal, with a little dried fish, and is, " in fact, the result of a calculation of the cheapest nutriment on which human life can be supported." (p. 429.)

" I have heard indeed," continues this enlightened traveller, " of the many luxuries the Negro might enjoy were he not too indolent; of the poultry and vegetables he might raise round his hut; but his unconquerable idleness masters all other feelings. I have seldom heard an argument against the Negroes that was not double-edged. If they are, indeed, so indolent by nature that even a regard for their own comforts proves insufficient to rouse them to exertion, with what colour can it be asserted that they feel it no misfortune to be compelled to daily labour for another? Is the sound of the whip so very exhilarating that it dispels at once indolence and suffering? But I admit the fact of their indolence. The human mind fits itself to its situation, and to the demands which are made upon its energies. Cut off hope for the future and freedom for the present; superadd a due pressure of bodily suffering and personal degradation; and you have a slave, who, of whatever zone, nation, or complexion, will be, what the poor African is, torpid, debased, and lowered beneath the standard of humanity.

" To inquire if, so circumstanced, he is happy, would be a question idly ridiculous, except that the affirmative is not only gravely maintained, but constitutes an essential moral prop of the whole slave system. Neither they who affirm, nor they who deny, pretend to any talisman by which the feelings of the heart may be set in open day; but if general reasoning be resorted to, since pain and pleasure are found to be the necessary result of the operation of certain accidents on the human constitution, the aggregate of our sensations (that is, our happiness or misery) must be allowed to depend on the number and combination of these accidents. ' If you prick us, do we not bleed? If you tickle us, do we not laugh? If you poison us, do we not die?'

" Should there be any unknown principle in the Negro's constitution which enables him to convert natural effects into their contraries, and so despise contingencies whether of good or evil, he may pride himself in having over-past the glory both of saints and stoics; but the fact would no more justify his oppressors, than did the stubborn endurance of Epictetus the barbarity of his master, who broke his leg. It would be too much, first to inflict a cruelty, and then to take credit for the patience with which it is supported: but the fact itself is, in this case, more than doubtful. That to a certain point the feelings of the slave grow callous under bondage, may be conceded: this is the mercy of Nature: but that they are wholly extinguished by suffering, is contradicted by facts of too palpable evidence; one of which is, that it is no uncommon thing for Negroes to commit suicide. This I heard from a gentleman of Charleston; and I have since met with the still more unexceptionable testimony of a friend to the slave trade.

" Dr. Williamson, in his ' Medical and Miscellaneous Observations relative to the West India Islands,' observes : ' Negroes anticipate that they will, upon death removing them from that country, be restored to their native land, and enjoy their friends' society in a future state. The ill-disposed to their masters will sometimes be guilty of suicide; or by a resolute determination resort to dirt-eating, and thence produce disease, and at length death.' (i. 93.) This is the kind of man who, should he ever hear of the death of Cato, would call it the result of ' an ill disposition towards his master, Cæsar.'

" I remember to have once heard a person assert, from his own experience, that a cargo of Africans expressed great pleasure on finding themselves made slaves, on their arrival in America. A further explanation, however, removed the seeming improbability of this anecdote. They imagined they had been purchased for the purpose of being eaten, and therefore rejoiced in their ignorance, when they discovered they were only to be held in bondage." Hall, pp. 429—432.

It is impossible to resist the force of this reasoning. It may be evaded by sophistry or opposed by selfishness, or questioned by prejudice or ignorance, but its truth and justice will be self-evident to the mind of every intelligent and candid observer. The consideration of this terrific subject very naturally leads our ingenious author to inquire how it has happened that " slavery and slave dealing," though exhibiting little either in speculation or practice, which is calculated to convince the judgement or captivate the affections, should have found advocates, not merely among slave-traders and slave-holders, but among men of cultivated, and apparently liberal, minds. Without any natural sympathy with cruelty, and without any interest in the question, they still defend these hideous practices, as if they were worthy of being embraced and cherished for the sake of their own native loveliness. Many of them would shudder at inflicting on a single fellow-creature a particle of the privations and sufferings, which they nevertheless uphold in argument as fit "to be the portion and daily bread of thousands." We shall, at present, abstain from entering on this extensive and inviting chapter in the history of the human mind, and content ourselves with noticing Mr. Hall's explanation of the fact which has so justly surprised him. He refers it to the influence of authority, to prejudice, or to an inaptitude to investigate any subject beyond the line of their ordinary occupations.

" As such persons scarcely affect to reason, or inquire, it is difficult to discover on what grounds they rest their opinions : the few who pretend to speak from experience, have seldom more to urge than the experience of good West India dinners ; and how can any thing be wrong where people dine so well ? The many, who have made up their minds by mere dint of not thinking on the matter, take fast hold upon some one of the many bold falsehoods, or skilful sophisms, with which those interested in the traffic are ever ready to furnish such as find it troublesome, or fancy it unsafe, to use their own understandings ;—as for instance—' Negro slaves are better off than the poorer classes in many European countries. They are quite contented with their situation, except when perverted by their pretended friends. It is the proprietor's interest to use them well, and therefore he does use them well. Or, The abolitionists are methodists, jacobins, or enthusiasts, and therefore unfit to be trusted with reforms of any kind ; besides, slavery has existed time out of mind, and why is the present generation to pretend to more wisdom and humanity than their forefathers ?' Their very good nature leads them to disbelieve most of the cruelties they hear related as connected with the slave system ; or should the evidence of particular facts occasionally overpower their prejudice, they readily admit, that as Negroes are constitutionally different from White men, they require a different treatment ; so that what may seem harsh to us, and would in fact be harsh to people of our complexion, is no more to them than a salubrious regimen. Such advocates, however contemptible as logicians, are of great numerical importance. They constitute the standing army of corruption in all shapes; are always to be found among the supporters of power, and may be depended on as the steady friends of whatever is established. To the efforts of the enlightened few, they oppose the inert resistance of impassive matter; a resistance which gains respect by seeming disinterested, and remains unassailable, because, like the tortoise, it presents no vital point of attack. Self-interest takes the field with better armour, and more enterprise; but the combat would be short-lived, did he not, after each discomfiture, find refuge within the shell of his simple ally." Hall, pp. 417—419.

In the United States, indeed, as Mr. Hall admits, the influence of these causes is less powerful than in Europe. In America, few can be uninformed of the actual condition of the slaves; and as they are accustomed thoroughly to discuss all public questions, the case of the Black population has a better chance of being at least understood by them than by us. Accordingly, in some of the old States, and in all which have recently been admitted into the Union, slavery has been formally excluded from their constitution. The whole of the Eastern and a great part of the Central States, and many enlightened individuals even in the southern provinces, particularly the Quakers, are declared enemies of the system of slavery. It is true, that, for the most part, they oppose it rather as a great political evil, than as a violation of the eternal obligation of humanity and justice: nevertheless, its extent is in this way gradually narrowing. With them there is no dispute, nor, indeed, can there be, respecting the opprobrious and humiliating facts of the case. With us, on the contrary, the only persons who, in general, have an opportunity of viewing with their own eyes the state of colonial bondage, are persons interested in upholding it. And they are induced by tenderness for their own reputation, as well as by the strong feeling of interest, and, we may add, by pride, to throw a veil over the enormities of the system, and to resist every attempt to withdraw it. The advantage which America possesses in this important respect, would encourage a hope of the eventual extinction of this evil at no very distant period, at least, at an earlier period than it would be reasonable to expect it in our own colonial possessions, but for another circumstance on which Mr. Hall, incidentally, but feelingly, touches, and which must have a powerful influence in perpetuating the miseries of slavery in the United States ; we mean, the force of habit. Let any one consider, for a moment, the different sensations with which an individual who had never witnessed the infliction of a wound, and a practised surgeon, would regard the amputation of a limb ;—or the disgust which would be excited in an inhabitant of some splendid mansion in Grosvenor Square, on being admitted, for the first time, to the occupancy of an apartment in the Borough Compter or Bristol Jail, as compared with the feelings of some old offender who was familiar with all the filth and abominations of the place. A similar difference will be found to exist in the feelings of the man who has a near view of slavery for the first time, and of him whose eye has become familiar with its horrors, or has, perhaps, been accustomed to them from infancy. It cannot be expected that a person born and educated in Carolina, or in Jamaica, should be shocked by those parts of the slave system, which, if viewed by a person of common sensibility for the first time, would fill him with disgust and horror. In one respect, therefore, we are more advantageously situated in this country than in America for judging accurately of the effects of the slave system. The natural feelings which they are calculated to excite are less blunted by familiarity. These remarks are illustrated by what Mr. Hall tells us of the impression he received, when, in travelling southward from Philadelphia, he first entered the slave States.

" The houses, universally shaded with large virandas, seem to give notice of a southern climate ; the huts round them, open to the elements, and void of every intention of comfort, tell a less pleasing tale : they inform the traveller he has entered upon a land of masters and slaves, and he beholds the scene marred with wretched dwellings and wretched faces. The eye, which for the first time looks on a slave, feels a painful impression : he is one for whom the laws of humanity are reversed, who has known nothing of society but its injustice, nothing of his fellow-man but his hardened, undisguised, atrocious selfishness. The cowering humility, the expressions of servile respect, with which the Negro approaches the White man, strike on the senses, not like the courtesy of the French and Italian peasant, giving a grace to Poverty, but with the chilling indication of a crushed spirit: the sound of the lash is in his accents of submission; and the eye which shrinks from mine, caught its fear from that of the task-master. Habit steels us to all things; and it is not to be expected that objects, constantly present, should continue to excite the same sensations which they cause when looked upon for the first time,— and this, perhaps, is one reason why so much cruelty has been tolerated in the world: but whosoever should look on a slave for the first time in his life, with the same indifferent gaze he would bestow on any casual object, may triumph in the good fortune through which he was born free, but in his heart he is a slave, and, as a moral being, degraded infinitely below the Negro, in whose soul the light of freedom has been extinguished, not by his own insensibility, but by the tyranny of others. Did the miserable condition of the Negro leave him mind for reflection, he might laugh in his chains to see how slavery has stricken the land with ugliness. The smiling villages, and happy population of the Eastern and Central States, give place to the splendid equipages of a few planters, and a wretched Negro population, crawling among filthy hovels—for villages (after crossing the Susquehanna) there are scarcely any; there are only plantations: the very name speaks volumes." Hall, pp. 318—320.

Let us observe, on the other hand, the effect produced by the force of habit on the moral feelings of a respectable individual, Mr. Duff; a person residing in a remote valley in the state of Virginia, whom Mr. Hall describes as an excellent specimen of the best part of his neighbours. He was remarkably temperate; never uttered an immoral expression; and his disposition seemed in a high degree friendly and benevolent.

" Yet, mark," observes our author, " the withering effect of slavery on the moral feelings! he was talking of the different ways men had in that part of the country of making money. ' Some,' said he, ' purchase droves of hogs, oxen, or horses, in one part of the Union, and drive them for sale to another; and some buy Negroes in the same way, and drive them, chained together, to different markets: I expect two gentlemen here this evening with a drove.' I expressed my horror of such traffic: he civilly assented to my observation, but plainly without any similar feeling, and spoke of the gentlemen he expected as if they were just as ' honourable men' as any other fair dealers in the community : luckily I was not cursed with their company. I never chanced to fall in with one of these human droves; but I borrow from a pleasing little work, written by a Virginian, and entitled, ' Letters from Virginia,' the following description which he gives, in the character of a foreigner newly landed at Norfolk :—

" ' I took the boat this morning, and crossed the ferry over to Portsmouth, the small town which I told you is opposite to this place. It was court day, and a large crowd of people was gathered about the door of the court-house. I had hardly got upon the steps to look in, when my ears were assailed by the voice of singing, and turning round to discover from what quarter it came, I saw a group of about thirty Negroes, of different sizes and ages, following a rough-looking White man, who sat carelessly lolling in his sulky. They had just turned round the corner, and were coming up the main street to pass by the spot where I stood, on their way out of town. As they came nearer I saw some of them loaded with chains to prevent their escape ; while others had hold of each other's hands, strongly grasped, as if to support themselves in their affliction. I particularly noticed a poor mother, with an infant sucking at her breast as she walked along, while two small children had hold of her apron on either side, almost running to keep up with the rest. They came along singing a little wild hymn, of sweet and mournful melody, flying, by a divine instinct of the heart, to the consolation of religion, the last refuge of the unhappy, to support them in their distress. The sulky now stopped before the tavern, at a little distance beyond the court-house, and the driver got out. " My dear sir," said I to a person who stood near me, " can you tell me what these poor people have been doing? what is their crime? and what is to be their punishment?" " O," said he, " it is nothing at all, but a parcel of Negroes sold to Carolina; and that man is their driver, who has bought them." " But what have they done, that they should be sold into banishment?" " Done!" said he : " nothing at all that I know of : their masters wanted money, I suppose, and these drivers give good prices." Here the driver, having supplied himself with brandy, and his horse with water (the poor Negroes of course wanted nothing), stepped into his chair again, cracked his whip and drove on, while the miserable exiles followed in funeral procession behind him." " Hall, pp. 357—360.

The view which Mr. Hall has given of the slavery of the United States is substantially confirmed by Mr. Fearon, who states " the treatment of the Negroes throughout these states" to be " as villainous as can well be imagined." (p. 268.) He has given us a transcript of some of the provisions of a law, not an ancient and now obsolete law, but a law passed by the city council of New Orleans, the capital of Louisiana, on the 17th day of October, 1817, for the government of the slave population.

By this law, any slave found occupying, or sleeping in, any house, out-house, building, or inclosure, not his owner's or immediate employer's, without a ticket from such owner or employer, expressly describing the place, and specifying the time for which the license is granted, shall be committed to gaol by any officer of police, or any other White person, *there to receive twenty lashes*, on a warrant from the mayor or justice of the peace, unless his owner or master shall previously pay five dollars for him, with all costs.

The sixth clause of this Act confines assemblies of slaves for dancing or other merriment exclusively to Sundays, and to such open and public places as the mayor shall appoint ; such assemblies not to continue later than sun-set : every violation of the rule to be punished with ten to twenty-five lashes, besides being liable to the penalties of the preceding clause.

The four following clauses, which we give entire, will sufficientl satisfy our readers of the humanity of this modern *Code Noir*.

" No person giving a ball to Free People of Colour shall, on any pretext, admit or suffer to be admitted to said ball any slave, on penalty of a fine from ten to fifty dollars ; and any slave admitted to any such ball shall receive fifteen lashes.

" Every slave, except such as may be blind or infirm, who shall walk in any street or open place with a cane, club, or other stick, shall be carried to the police gaol, where he shall receive twenty-five lashes, and shall moreover forfeit every such cane, club, or other stick, to any White person seizing the same ; and every slave carrying any arms whatever, shall be punished in the manner prescribed by the Black Code of this State.

" If any slave shall be guilty of whooping or hallooing any where
in the city or suburbs, or of making any clamorous noise, or of
singing aloud any indecent song, he or she shall, for each and every
such offence, receive at the police gaol, on a warrant from the
mayor, or any justice of peace, the number of twenty lashes or
stripes ; and if any such offence be committed on board any vessel,
the master or commander thereof shall forfeit and pay a sum of
twenty dollars for each and every such offence.

" Every slave who shall be guilty of disrespect towards any
White person, or shall insult any Free person, shall receive thirty
lashes, upon an order from the mayor, or justice of the peace."
Fearon, pp. 277, 278.

If the subject were not too serious for mirth, there is something
perfectly ludicrous in these legislative enactments.   They are only
to be explained on the principle to which we have already referred.
We are familiar in private life with the strange effects which often
proceed from terror when it has once taken full possession of the
mind ; the laughable exaggerations and irrational expedients to
which it leads.   Here, however, its unrestrained influence com-
promises the comfort and happiness of whole communities, and
that not for a passing moment, but for ages, and throughout the
miserable succession of generations yet unborn.

A practical proof of the wretchedness and degradation, to which
this unhappy class of our fellow-creatures is reduced, is exhibited,
we are told, at " every tavern" in the slave states; where, Mr.
Hall informs us, advertisements are seen posted for runaway slaves.
" The barbarous phraseology in which they were drawn up sometimes amused" him ; but he was more frequently disgusted with
" the ferocious spirit of revenge" they too plainly expressed.   An
incident, which we quote from Mr. Fearon, speaks the same painful
truth still more strongly.   The scene is laid at Lawes' hotel at
Middletown, in the state of Kentucky.

" A few minutes before dinner, my attention was excited by the
piteous cries of a human voice accompanied with the loud cracking
of a whip.   Following the sound, I found that it issued from a log-
barn, the door of which was fastened.   Peeping through the logs,
I perceived the bar-keeper of the tavern, together with a stout
man, more than six feet high, who was called colonel ————,
and a Negro boy about 14 years of age, stript naked, receiving

the lashes of these monsters, who *relieved* each other in the use of a horsewhip; the poor boy fell down upon his knees several times, begging and praying that they would not kill him, and that he would do any thing they liked; this produced no cessation in their exercise. At length Mr. Lawes, the master of the hotel, arrived, told the valiant colonel and his humane employer, the bar-keeper, to desist, and that the boy's refusal to cut wood was in obedience to his (Mr. L.'s) directions. Colonel ———— said, that ' he did not know what the Niggar had done, but that the bar-keeper requested his assistance to whip Cæsar; of course he lent him a hand, being no more than he should expect Mr. Lawes to do for him under similar circumstances. At table Mr. Lawes said, that he had not been so vexed for seven years. This expression gave me pleasure, and also afforded me, as I thought, an opportunity to reprobate the general system of slavery; but not one voice joined with mine: each gave vent in the following language to the super-abundant quantity of the milk of human kindness, with which their breasts were overflowing:—

" ' I guess he deserved all he got.'

" ' It would have been of small account if the Niggar had been whipt to death.'

" ' I always serve my Niggars that way: there is nothing else so good for them.'

" It appeared that this boy was the property of a regular slave-dealer, who was then absent at Natchez with a cargo. Mr. Lawes' humanity fell lamentably in my estimation when he stated, ' that whipping Niggars, if they were his own, was perfectly right, and they always deserved it; but what made him mad was, that the boy was left under his care by a friend, and he did not like to have a friend's property injured.'

" There is in this instance of the treatment of a Negro, nothing that in this State is at all singular; and much as I condemned New York, Pennsylvania, and Ohio, when in those sections, I must now give them the character of enlightened humanity, compared with this State, in which such conduct as that I have described, is tolerated and approved." Fearon, pp. 239—241.

The following relation, however, of Mr. Hall, is of a still more affecting description. It is an account which he has given us of the trial and execution of a Negro, that took place during his stay in Charleston, South Carolina.

" A man died on board a merchant ship, apparently in consequence of poison mixed with the dinner served up to the ship's company. The cabin-boy and cook were suspected, because they were, from their occupations, the only persons on board who did not partake of the mess, the effects of which began to appear as soon as it was tasted. As the offence was committed on the high seas, the cook, though a Negro, became entitled to the benefit of a jury, and, with the cabin-boy, was put on his trial. The boy, a fine-looking lad, and wholly unabashed by his situation, was readily acquitted. The Negro's turn was next. He was a man of low stature, ill-shapen, and with a countenance singularly disgusting. The proofs against him were, first, that he was cook ; so who else could have poisoned the mess ? It was indeed overlooked, that two of the crew had absconded since the ship came into port. Secondly, he had been heard to utter expressions of ill-humour before he went on board : that part of the evidence indeed was suppresed which went to explain these expressions. The real proof, however, was written in his skin, and in the uncouth lines of his countenance. He was found guilty.

" Mr. Crafts, junior, a gentleman of the Charleston bar, who, from motives of humanity, had undertaken his defence, did not think a man ought to die for his colour, albeit it was the custom of the country ; and moved in consequence for a new trial, on the ground of partial and insufficient evidence ; but the Judge, who had urged his condemnation with a vindictive earnestness, intrenched himself in forms, and found the law gave him no power in favour of mercy. He then forwarded a representation of the case to the President, through one of the senators of the State ; but the senator ridiculed the idea of interesting himself for the life of a Negro, who was therefore left to his cell and the hangman. In this situation he did not, however, forsake himself ; and it was now, when prejudice and persecution had spent their last arrow on him, that he seemed to put on his proper nature, to vindicate not only his innocence, but the moral equality of his race, and those mental energies which the White man's pride would deny to the shape of his head and the woolliness of his hair. Maintaining the most undeviating tranquillity, he conversed with ease and cheerfulness, whenever his benevolent counsel, who continued his kind attentions to the last, visited his cell. I was present on one of these occasions, and observed his tone and manner, neither sullen nor desperate, but quiet and resigned, suggesting whatever occurred to him on the circumstances of his own case, with as much calmness as if he had been uninterested in the event; yet as if he deemed it a duty to omit none of the means placed within his reach for vindicating his innocence. He had constantly attended the exhortations of a Methodist preacher, who, for conscience sake, visited ' those who were in prison;' and, having thus strengthened his spirit with religion, on the morning of his execution, breakfasted, as usual, heartily; but before he was led out, he requested permission to address a few words of advice to the companions of his captivity. ' I have observed much in them,' he added, ' which requires to be amended, and the advice of a man in my situation may be respected.' A circle was accordingly formed in his cell, in the midst of which he seated himself, and addressed them at some length, with a sober and collected earnestness of manner, on the profligacy which he had noted in their behaviour, while they had been fellow-prisoners; recommending to them the rules of conduct prescribed by that religion in which he now found his support and consolation.

" Certainly, if we regard the quality and condition of the actors only, there is an infinite distance betwixt this scene and the parting of Socrates with his disciples: should we, however, put away from our thoughts such differences as are merely accidental, and seize that point of coincidence which is most interesting and important; namely, the triumph of mental energy over the most clinging weaknesses of our nature, the Negro will not appear wholly unworthy of a comparison with the sage of Athens. The latter occupied an exalted station in the public eye; though persecuted even unto death and ignominy by a band of triumphant despots, he was surrounded in his last moments by his faithful friends and disciples, to whose talents and affection he might safely trust the vindication of his fame, and the unsullied whiteness of his memory he knew that his hour of glory must come, and that it would not pass away The Negro had none of these aids, he was a man friendless and despised; the sympathies of society were locked up against him; he was to atone for an odious crime by an ignominious death; the consciousness of his innocence was confined to his own bosom, there probably to sleep for ever; to the rest of mankind he was a wretched criminal, an object, perhaps, of contempt and detestation, even to the guilty companions of his prison-house; he had no philosophy with which to reason down those natural misgivings, which may be supposed to precede the violent dissolution of life and body; he could make no appeal to posterity to reverse an unjust judgement. To have borne all this patiently would have been much; he bore it heroically.

" Having ended his discourse, he was conducted to the scaffold, where having calmly surveyed the crowds collected to witness his fate, he requested leave to address them. Having obtained permission, he stept firmly to the edge of the scaffold, and having commanded silence by his gestures, ' You are come,' said he, ' to be spectators of my sufferings; you are mistaken, there is not a person in this crowd but suffers more than I do. I am cheerful and contented, for I am innocent.' He then observed, that he truly forgave all those who had taken any part in his condemnation, and believed that they had acted conscientiously from the evidence before them; and disclaimed all idea of imputing guilt to any one. He then turned to his counsel, who, with feelings which honoured humanity, had attended him to the scaffold: ' To you, Sir,' said he, ' I am indeed most grateful; had you been my son, you could not have acted by me more kindly:' and observing his tears, he continued, ' This, Sir, distresses me beyond any thing I have felt yet; I entreat you will feel no distress on my account, I am happy.' Then praying to Heaven to reward his benevolence, he took leave of him, and signified his readiness to die, but requested he might be excused from having his eyes and hands bandaged; wishing, with an excusable pride, to give this final proof of his unshaken firmness; he, however, submitted on this point to the representations of the sheriff, and died without the quivering of a muscle.

" The spectators, who had been drawn together, partly by idle curiosity, and partly by a detestation of his supposed crime, retired with tears for his fate, and execrations on his murderers." Hall, pp. 433—438.

We might fairly challenge the writers of romance to rival this story in depth of interest. We should only weaken its effect by any comments of our own.

The depressed and degraded condition of the Negro slave is communicated, as might be expected, by an almost infallible contagion, to the whole of the free Black and Coloured population of the United States. Nor are even those parts of the Union, called, by way of distinction, Free States, in which slavery is abolished by law, exempt from this charge. The curse of slavery pursues the descendants of slaves to the latest generation. So long as the slightest tinge of African blood can be discovered to flow in their veins, however professedly liberal the institutions of any particular state may chance to be, the sentence of civil disability and degradation continues in force. There exists, as Mr. Fearon well expresses it, in *all* these states, *not excepting any,* "a penal law deeply written in the *minds* of the whole White population, which subjects their Coloured fellow-citizens to unconditional contumely and never-ceasing insult. No respectability, however unquestionable ; no property, however large ; no character, however unblemished, will gain a man, whose body is, in American estimation, *cursed* with even a twentieth portion of the blood of his African ancestry, admission into society. They are considered as mere Pariahs, as outcasts and vagrants on the face of the earth." These persons, though many of them are possessed of the rights of citizenship, it would be little to say, are not admitted to the exercise of their civil franchises ; they are not admitted to a participation of the same religious privileges. We are told by the Abbé du Bois, in his account of the Hindoos, as well as by Dr. C. Buchanan, in his Christian Researches, that the transcendent greatness of Juggernaut levels all distinctions among his votaries ; and that Bramins and Soodras are, in his presence, melted down into one common state of prostration and abasement. In Christian America, the case is different. The god whom they worship is not the God who is " no respecter of persons," and who " hath made of one blood all nations of men." Even in Philadelphia and New York, there are " African churches" appropriated to " those native Americans who are Black, or have any shade of colour darker than White." Though nominally citizens, they " are not admitted into the churches which are visited by Whites." (p. 167.) In perfect conformity with this spirit, observes Mr. Fearon, is the fact that, in New York, the most degraded White will not walk the street with a Negro ; so that although New York is a free state, it is so only on parchment, the Black and Coloured Americans being practically and politically slaves : thus showing, that "the laws of the mind, are, after all, infinitely more strong and more effective than those of the statute book." p. 61.

The following anecdote will throw some further light on this subject : —

"Soon after landing at New York," says Mr. Fearon, "I called at a hair-dresser's in Broadway, nearly opposite the city-hall. The man in the shop was a Negro. He had nearly finished with me, when a Black man, very respectably dressed, came into the shop, and sat down. The barber inquired if he wanted the proprietor or his boss (master), as he termed him, who was also a Black ; the answer was in the negative, but that he wished to have his hair cut. My man turned upon his heel, and, with the greatest contempt, muttered in a tone of proud importance, 'We do not cut Coloured men here, Sir.' The poor fellow walked out without replying, exhibiting in his countenance confusion, humiliation, and mortification. I immediately requested, that if the refusal was on account of my being present, he might be called back. The hairdresser was astonished : 'You cannot be in earnest, Sir,' he said. I assured him that I was so, and that I was much concerned in witnessing the refusal from no other cause than that his skin was of a darker tinge than my own. He stopped the motion of his scissars : and after a pause of some seconds, in which his eyes were fixed upon my face, he said, 'Why, I guess as how, Sir, what you say is mighty elegant, and you're an elegant man ; but I guess you are not of these parts.'—'I am from England,' said I, 'where we have neither so cheap nor so enlightened a Government, as yours, but we have no slaves.'—'Aye, I guessed you were not raised here : you salt-water people are mighty grand to Coloured people ; you are not so proud, and I guess you have more to be proud of : now I reckon you do not know that my boss would not have a single ugly or clever gentleman come to his store, if he cut Coloured men : now my boss, I guess, ordered me to turn out every Coloured man from the store right away ; and if I did not, he would send me off slick ; for the slimmest gentleman in York would not come to his store if Coloured men were let in. But you know all that, Sir, I guess, without my telling you : you are an elegant gentleman too, Sir.' I assured him that I was ignorant of the fact which he stated; but which, from the earnestness of his manner, I concluded must be true." pp. 58, 59.

" At the dinner-table I commenced a relation of this occurrence to three American gentlemen, one of whom was a doctor, the others were in the law : they were men of education and of liberal opinions. When I arrived at the point of the Black being turned out, they exclaimed, ' Aye, right, perfectly right : I would never go to a barber's where a Coloured man was cut !' Observe, these gentlemen were not from the south ; they are residents of New York, and I believe were born there." Fearon, p. 60.

But let us listen to the testimony of Mr. Hall on the same subject. He is speaking of Carolina. There, he says, the condition of a free Man of Colour is, in fact, scarcely preferable to that of a slave.

" Subjected to the same mode of trial, exposed to the same jealous surveillance, carefully excluded from all the rights and privileges of citizenship, and surrounded by every kind of snares, both legal and illegal, his freedom seems but a mockery superadded to oppression. The statute declares, that every Man of Colour shall be presumed a slave : every newspaper is a commentary on the injustice and barbarity of this enactment ; every day Men of Colour are advertised as taken up on suspicion of being slaves : they are committed to jail, and, if no owner appears, are sold to pay expenses. But the direct operation of the law is not all the free Man of Colour has to dread.

" The humane exertions of some gentlemen of the Charleston bar have lately brought to light a singular system for kidnapping free Negroes, and selling them as slaves into Kentucky, or any state at a distance from their connections. The agents were a justice of the peace, a constable, and a slave-dealer.

" The process was as simple as unblushing villainy could devise. A victim having been selected, one of the firm applied to the Justice, upon a sham charge of assault, or similar offence, for a writ, which was immediately issued and served by the constable, and the Negro conveyed to prison. Here, without friends or money, he is to await his trial for some unknown crime charged against him by some unknown accuser : no wonder if, in this desolate condition, his spirits sink, and his fears anticipate the worst : the constable now appears, exaggerates the dangers of his situation; explains how small is his chance of being liberated, even if innocent, by reason of the amount of the jail fees and other legal expenses; but he knows a worthy man who is interested in his behalf, and will do what is necessary to procure his freedom, upon no harder condition than an engagement to serve him for a certain number of years. It may be supposed, the Negro is persuaded; 'influenced, perhaps, (as the counsel for the defendants observed on the trial,) by the charms of a country life.' The worthy slave-dealer now appears on the stage. The indenture of bondage is ratified in presence of the worthy magistrate and constable, who share the price of blood, and the victim is hurried on ship-board to be seen no more.

"This traffic had been long carried on, when humanity discovered and exposed it in a court of justice: but since, by the present law, there is no such offence as man-stealing, it could be punished as false imprisonment only. Should not, however, the shame of discovery produce a stronger impression on the parties engaged in this iniquitous traffic, than can be expected from their depraved habits, it is more than probable it will continue to be carried on with keener and perhaps more atrocious dexterity than before." Hall, pp. 424—426.

Let it not, however, be supposed that the Black and Coloured race alone experience the pernicious consequences of the prevalence of slavery. The *curse* has reached beyond them, and the moral debasement which it has engendered in the minds of the chief actors in this drama of guilt and blood—in the minds of the masters of slaves, furnishes a striking comment on that passage of Holy Writ; "They shall eat of the fruit of their own way, and be filled with their own devices." Is it possible for any serious mind to read the following extracts without acknowledging the righteous government and retributive justice of the Almighty?

"The existence of slavery in the United States has a most visible effect upon the national character. It necessarily brutalizes the minds of the southern and western inhabitants; it lowers, indeed, the tone of humane and correct feeling throughout the Union; and imperceptibly contributes to the existence of that great difference which here exists between theory and practice." Fearon, pp. 378, 379.

Mr. Hall gives his opinion upon the subject somewhat more at length :—

" It is impossible to consider the character of the southern states, without again adverting to the pernicious effects of slavery.

" Land cultivated by slaves requires a considerable capital, and will therefore be divided among a small number of proprietors. Experience, too, shows that the quantity of labour performed by slaves is much below that of an equal number of free cultivators : the number of persons deriving support from the soil will consequently be less ; but the loss is not in quantity only, the quality is proportionably deteriorated. He who commands the sweat of others, will be little inclined to toil himself* ; the inclination will diminish with the necessity. The fact is so consonant with this remark, that in the southern states, the fisheries, and all branches of active exertion, fall into the hands of the New Englanders : so much so, that the city of Charleston is supplied with fish by smacks from Marble-head and Boston. Climate might be supposed to have a partial influence in producing this effect, were not such individuals as are compelled by the nature of their occupations to rely much on their own efforts found no ways inferior, in attainments and application, to the same description of persons in the more temperate portions of the Union. Nay, have not almost all the sultriest regions of the globe been alternately the seats of sloth and enterprize ?

" The same distribution of property which renders labour unnecessary to its proprietor, is no less fatal to his mental improvement. Experience informs us, that means and leisure are less powerful excitements to study than the spur of necessity, and the hope of profit. Information will be first sought, that it may be useful ; it will afterwards be pursued for the pleasure of the acquisition only. The planter has, therefore, been ever reckoned amongst the least enlightened members of society ; But, says a proverb, those whom the devil finds idle, he sets about his own work. Dissipation must be always the resource of the unoccupied and ill-instructed.

" If the political effects of slavery are pernicious to the citizen, its moral effects are still more fatal to the man. 'There must doubt-

---

* "' Of the proprietors of slaves, a very small proportion, indeed, are ever seen to labour.' Jefferson's Notes, p. 241."

less' (says Mr. Jefferson) ' be an unhappy influence on the manners of the people, produced by the existence of slavery among us. The whole commerce between master and slave is a perpetual exercise of the most boisterous passions; the most unremitting despotism on the one part, and degrading submission on the other. Our children see this, and learn to imitate it, for man is an imitative animal. The parent storms, the child looks on, catches the lineaments of wrath, puts on the same airs in the circle of smaller slaves, gives loose to the worst of passions; and thus nursed, educated, and daily exercised in tyranny, cannot but be stamped by it with odious peculiarities. The man must be a prodigy who can retain his morals and manners undepraved by such circumstances.' Notes, p. 241.

" We know the time of prodigies is past, and that natural effects will follow their causes. The manners of the lower classes in the Southern States are brutal and depraved *. Those of the upper, corrupted by power, are frequently arrogant and assuming : unused to restraint or contradiction of any kind, they are necessarily quarrelsome ; and in their quarrels, the native ferocity of their hearts breaks out. Duelling is not only in general vogue and fashion, but is practised with circumstances of peculiar vindictiveness. It is usual when two persons have agreed to fight, for each to go out regularly and practise at a mark, in the presence of their friends, during the interval which precedes their meeting : one of the parties, therefore, commonly falls.

" Did the whole of the above causes operate with undiminished influence, the result would be horrible ; but there are several circumstances continually working in mitigation of those evils." Hall, pp. 457, 460.

The testimony which we have here adduced, has received the most decisive confirmation from another, and, it will be thought by some, a less suspicious, quarter. Mr. Morris Birkbeck, both in his " Notes on a Journey in America," and in his " Letters from the Illinois," appears to have laboured to convey to his countrymen a favourable impression, not only of the United States as a scene of

---

* " The stage-drivers, for instance, are more inhuman, and much inferior in decency of behaviour to the Negroes, who are sometimes employed in the same capacity ; so that it seems not improbable, that the effects of slavery, upon the lower orders at least, are more debasing to the governing class, than to the governed."

profitable enterprize, but of the general character and manners of its inhabitants. But what is his representation of the nature of slavery, and its effects on the moral and intellectual qualities of the American population? Let the friends and advocates of our slave-system, and, above all, let our members of Parliament, who may be called to revise that system, weigh it well. It is replete with considerations of momentous import. The passage will be found in Birk-beck's " Notes," p. 20.

" May 10. I saw two female slaves and their children sold by auction in the street; an incident of common occurrence here, though horrifying to myself and many other strangers. I could hardly bear to see them handled and examined like cattle; and when I heard their sobs, and saw the big tears roll down their cheeks at the thoughts of being separated, I could not refrain from weeping with them. In selling these unhappy beings, little regard is had to the parting of the nearest relations. Virginia prides itself on the comparative mildness of its treatment of the slaves; and, in fact, they increase in numbers, many being annually supplied from this State to those further south, where the treatment is said to be much more severe. There are regular dealers who buy them up, and drive them in gangs, chained together, to a southern market. I am informed, that few weeks pass without some of them being marched through this place. A traveller told me, that he saw, two weeks ago, one hundred and twenty sold by auction in the streets of Richmond; and that they filled the air with their lamentations.

" It has also been confidently alleged, that the condition of slaves in Virginia, under the mild treatment they are said to experience. is preferable to that of our English labourers. I know and lament the degrading state of dependent poverty to which the latter have been gradually reduced by the operation of laws originally designed for their comfort and protection. I know also that many slaves pass their lives in comparative ease, and seem to be unconscious of their bonds, and that the *most wretched* of our paupers might envy the allotment of the *happy* Negro. This is not, however, instituting a fair comparison, to bring the opposite extremes of the two classes into competition. Let us take a view of some particulars which operate generally.

" In England, exertion is not the result of personal fear; in Virginia, it is the prevailing stimulus.

" The slave is punished for mere *indolence*, at the discretion of an *overseer*: the peasant is only punished by the law, when guilty of a crime.

" In England, the labourer and his employer are equal in the eye of the law : here the law affords the slave no protection, unless a White man gives testimony in his favour.

" Here, any White man may insult a Black with impunity; whilst the English peasant, should he receive a blow from his employer, might and would return it with interest, and afterwards have his remedy at law for the aggression.

" The testimony of a peasant weighs as much as that of a lord in a court of justice; but the testimony of a slave is never admitted at all in a case where a White man is opposed to him.

"A few weeks ago, in the streets of Richmond, a friend of mine saw a White boy wantonly throw quick-lime in the face of a Negro-man. The man shook the lime from his jacket, and some of it accidentally reached the eyes of the young brute. This casual retaliation excited the resentment of the brother of the boy, who complained to the slave's owner, and actually had him punished with thirty lashes. This would not have happened to an English peasant.

" I must, however, do this justice to the slave-master of Virginia : it was not from him that I ever heard a defence of slavery; some extenuation, on the score of expediency or necessity, is the utmost range now taken by that description of reasoners, who in former times would have attempted to support the principle as well as the practice.

" *Perhaps it is in its depraving influence on the moral sense of both slave and master, that slavery is most deplorable. Brutal cruelty, we may hope, is a rare and transient mischief; but the degradation of soul is universal.*

" *All America is now suffering in morals, through the baneful influence of Negro slavery, partially tolerated, corrupting justice at the very source.*

" Slavery," he says in another place, "that broadest, foulest blot which still prevails over so large a portion of the United States, will circumscribe my choice within narrow limits; for if political liberty be so precious, that to obtain it I can forgo the well-earned comforts of an English home, it must not be *to degrade and corrupt my children by the practice of slave-keeping.* This curse has taken fast hold of Kentucky, Tenessee, and all the new States to the South."

Such is the delineation of Negro slavery, as it exists in the United States, which has been given by three independent and impartial eye-witnesses. A writer in a contemporary Review, not remarkable for partiality to British in preference to trans-Atlantic policy, on contemplating the picture, expresses his keen indignation in terms which do him the highest honour. " The great curse of America," he observes, " is the institution of slavery, of itself far more than the foulest blot upon their national character, and an evil which counterbalances all the excisemen, licensers, and tax-gatherers of England. No virtuous man ought to trust his own character, or the character of his children, to the demoralizing effects produced by commanding slaves. Justice, gentleness, pity, and humility, soon give way before them. Conscience suspends its functions. The love of command, the impatience of restraint, get the better of every other feeling; and cruelty has no other limit than fear. That such feelings and such practices should exist among men who know the value of liberty, and profess to understand its principles, is the consummation of wickedness. Every American who loves his country should dedicate his whole life, and every faculty of his soul, to efface the foul stain from its character. If nations rank according to their wisdom and their virtue, what right has the American, a scourger and murderer of slaves, to compare himself with the least and lowest of the European nations ? *much more of this great and humane country*, where the greatest lord dares not lay a finger upon the meanest peasant ? What is freedom, where all are not free ; where the greatest of God's blessings is limited, with impious caprice, to the colour of the body ? And these are the men who taunt the English with their corrupt Parliament, with their buying and selling votes. Let the world judge which is the most liable to censure ;—we who, in the midst of our rottenness, have torn off the manacles of slaves all over the world ; or they who, with their idle purity and useless perfection, have remained mute and careless, while groans echoed and chains clanked round the very walls of their spotless Congress. We wish well to America, we rejoice in her prosperity, and are delighted to resist the absurd impertinence with which the character of her people is often treated in this country : but *the existence of slavery in America is an atro-*

cious crime, with which no measures can be kept, for which her situation affords no sort of apology, which makes liberty itself distrusted, and the boast of it disgusting." *Edinburgh Review,* No LXI. pp. 146—148.

This is just and spirited. Every reproach which the passage contains applies to the United States with an accuracy which admits of no cavil, and with a force which cannot be resisted. May it produce its due effect on the population of that rising empire! And may they be induced, while they yet may, to avert from themselves, by repentance and reformation, the judgements which, if the word of God be true, must sooner or later overtake such cruel and impious oppression! "The people of the land have used oppression, and have vexed the poor and needy, yea they have oppressed the stranger wrongfully. Therefore have I poured out mine indignation upon them: I have consumed them with the fire of my wrath. Their own way have I recompensed upon their heads, saith the Lord God." Ezek. xxii. 29.

There is, however, one circumstance in the extract we have given from the Edinburgh Review, which has not a little surprised us: we mean, that the reviewer should have chosen to place Great Britain in *contrast* with the United States on this occasion. We know not whether the writer intended that this part of his observations should be understood ironically. If so, he has failed of his aim. At the same time we admit, that a more severe and biting satire on this country could hardly be imagined than he has in effect conveyed by thus bringing her forward to darken the shade which he has thrown over the internal policy of America. In this view, every syllable he has uttered is wormwood and gall. Let our readers look back to the extract; and as they cast their eye over it a second time, let them substitute Great Britain for America, and then say whether every expression of vituperation, every term of reprobation and disgust, may not be applied with at least equal force and equal justice to the one country as to the other. Is the institution of slavery less a *curse* in Great Britain than in America? Is there something so peculiar in the moral atmosphere of a British colony, that the "justice, gentleness, pity, and humility," which wither elsewhere under the influence of slavery, should there flourish; that conscience should there retain its dominion, and prevent all the hideous effects so well described as the inevitable result of unmeasured despotism?—Is

" the value of liberty" less known, and are " its principles" less
understood in England than in America? Are " the feelings and
practices" involved in our system of colonial bondage less opposed
to those principles, or are they less " the consummation of wickedness," because they exist under the sanction of the British Government, rather than under that of the United States? *Is it less the
duty of every Englishman than of " every American, who loves
his country, to dedicate his whole life, and every faculty of his
soul, to efface this foul stain from its character?"* In " this great
and humane country" are there " no scourgers of slaves?" Can
we forget that " all are not free with us?" Or has the enfranchisement of our colonial bondsmen indeed taken place? And are those
laws at length abrogated in the British colonies, which, " with impious caprice, limit the greatest of God's blessings to the colour of
the body?" We have done much, it is true, to effect the universal
abolition of the *Slave-trade;* but what single legislative measure
have we, as a nation, yet adopted, not merely for " tearing off the
manacles" of our Black and Coloured fellow-subjects in the colonies, but for lightening the chains of their servitude, for protecting
them against oppression, for raising them in the scale of being?
The pathos of a few occasional speeches, the barren generalities of
an address to the Crown, the printing of reams of barbarous enactments, or horrid recitals, or studied apologies for slavery, will not
fulfil the obligations we are under to these wretched outcasts. It
may be true, that their groans do not echo, nor their chains clank,
around the walls of our Parliament, as around those of Congress:
but how many owners of slaves may be reckoned in the two branches
of our legislature, whose voice, during the last thirty years, may
possibly have assisted in preventing either the echo of the groan,
or the clank of the chain, from reaching our ears? But it has been
beyond the power of the loudest clamours either of interest or prejudice to drown them entirely; and the stifled sigh, the suppressed
but imploring murmur, have only pierced the deeper into the heart,
on account of the distance from which they have been wafted, and
the efforts made to obstruct their passage. But whether the British
Parliament catch the sound, or not, it has entered, doubtless, " into
the ears of the Lord of Sabaoth." And if it be true, as we do most
conscientiously believe it to be, that " *the existence of slavery in
America is an atrocious crime with which no measures can be kept,"*

is it possible for us to contemplate its existence within the British dominions in a less fearful light?

But we shall be told, that the slavery existing in our West Indian colonies differs materially in many respects from that which prevails in the United States. We do not mean to deny this. We believe that, in one or two particulars, the comparison might prove favourable to our own colonies. The slaves suffer less from cold in the West Indies than in America; and we do not mean to affirm that they are *excluded* from places of worship, however infrequently they may, in point of fact, attend them. In all the grand and essential points of personal comfort, however, the balance turns greatly on the other side. In America, they are in general more abundantly supplied with food. The labour of the field is there, too, for the most part, of a lighter kind than on sugar plantations. Task work is also more prevalent in America than in the West Indies, where labour is usually performed by gangs under the immediate impulse of the lash. Besides which, the Black and Coloured population have a readier access to the means of religious instruction in America than in our colonies *.

Our main purpose, in the present review, has been, by exhibiting a series of facts, to fix the value of certain general principles which apply to the state of Negro slavery in all parts of the civilized world, and to demonstrate that, in its leading characteristics, and more prominent tendencies and effects, it is, *when uncontrolled by some external influence* which shall make the emancipation of the slave the ultimate end of its regulations, the same revolting institution, whether administered by Spaniards or Portuguese, Frenchmen or Dutchmen, Englishmen or Americans.

* That the treatment of the slaves in the British colonies must be much more oppressive than it is even in the United States, would seem to be established beyond controversy by the following comparative statement of the Negro population of Jamaica and of the United States, in the years 1790 and 1820.

In 1790, the number of slaves in Jamaica is stated by Bryan Edwards at 250,000, which, however, he considered under-rated.

In 1810, from calculations founded on the Reports of the Assembly of Jamaica, they must have been about 320,000.—In 1817 they were rated, on what was affirmed to be a more accurate census, at 345,252, being an addition of only 95,252 in the whole of that period; and yet from the year 1787 to the period of the Abolition of the slave-trade in 1808, 188,785 appear to have been added by importation from Africa to the stock in that island, though the commencement of that importation is

four

The slavery of the African race, indeed, as it exists in the dominions of these nations, is accompanied by circumstances of degradation peculiar to itself, arising from the colour of the unhappy
subjects of it. Still the tendency to abuse the power with which
domestic slavery, under any form, necessarily invests the master,
is a principle which rests not on any modern discoveries, but which
comes to us upheld by the historical records of every succeeding
age. The only hope which can be indulged of effectually counter-
acting this tendency, is from the vigilant intervention of some
authority superior to that of the master, untainted with his prejudices, and uninfluenced by his selfish views. In the colonies of
Spain, for example, where the Government has exercised the entire
power of legislation, more has been done to alleviate the hardships
of Negro slavery, and to pave the way for its gradual extinction,
than in the colonies of any other nation. In the British colonies,
on the other hand, as well as in the United States of America,
where the makers of the laws are also the masters of the slaves,

four years prior to 1791; yet this will probably be counterbalanced by the admitted
inaccuracy of the returns in 1791.

In the year 1790, the slave population of the whole of the United States
was   -   -   -   -   -   -   -   -   676,696
In the year 1800 it was   -   -   -   -   -   -   894,444
In   -   1810   -   -   -   -   -   -   1,191,364
In   -   1820   -   -   -   -   -   -   1,531,431

The natural increase would have appeared to be considerably greater, if 174,142 had
not been added to the free Blacks during that period, about 100,000 of them by manumission.—We see that between 1790 and 1800 the rate of increase was $28\frac{1}{4}$ per cent.
Between 1800 and 1810   -   -   -   -   - $33\frac{3}{4}$ per cent.
And between 1810 and 1820   -   -   -   -   - $28\frac{1}{2}$ per cent.

The small difference in the increase from 1800 to 1810 must be attributed to the
partial importation from Africa during a short part of that period; but this will be
far more than counterbalanced by the number manumitted.

In 1790, then, Jamaica had a slave population of above   -   -   250,000
In 1817 and in 1820, (the number will probably be found nearly the
same in both years,)   -   -   -   -   -   -   345,252
In 1790, the United States' slave population was   -   -   676,696
In 1820,   ditto   ditto   -   -   -   -   1,531,431

If a system not more rigorous than the American system had been pursued in
Jamaica, the population of that island ought to have been in the year 1820, 565,775.

With 188,785 added by importation, still the population of Jamaica falls 220,523
short of what it ought to have been, making a difference altogether of 409,308. The
bare statement of such a waste of human life, such a cruel counteraction of the universal tendency of mankind to increase, renders all comment superfluous.

the legal constitution of slavery has been written in characters of blood, and hung round with all those attributes of cruelty and revenge which jealousy, contempt, and terror could suggest If in our own colonies, since the agitation of the Slave-trade controversy, the barbarous rigour of their earlier statute-books has been in some respects softened, may we not fairly ascribe the change to the influence of public opinion at home, operating on the fears of the masters of slaves, and forcing them to the reluctant adoption of enactments less revolting in their terms, and which, from their apparently humane bearing, might have the effect of averting the dreaded intervention of the imperial legislature? But if this view of the subject be correct, and in whatever degree it is so, the written law will be apt to fail of its effect, and to be at variance with the general practice, unless a very vigilant and efficient superintendence over its execution shall be exercised by the supreme authorities of the State. Hence arises the strong moral obligation of parliamentary interference for the protection of the servile population in our colonies, for restraining and punishing the abuse of the master's power, and for gradually but effectually putting an end to slavery itself. And although slavery, in existing circumstances, cannot, perhaps, be eradicated but by cautious and progressive measures, yet surely by means of judicious regulations, vigorously executed and vigilantly enforced, it might be divested in the interval of at least a part of its malignity.

Let it not, however, be supposed that we mean to prefer against the West Indians, as a body, any charge of extraordinary criminality, or to intimate that they are peculiar objects of public reprehension. It is not so much *they* who are in fault, as the system with which they are, in many, perhaps in most, cases, involuntarily connected. It is their misfortune to have been born, perhaps, in a slave colony, and to have been familiarized with the view of slavery from the moment of their birth. It would be to exact from such persons something more than we are entitled to look for, something more than is consistent with the ordinary phenomena of human nature, were we, in their case, to regard as a mark of singular depravity or inhumanity the circumstance of their differing, in their feelings and habits of thinking on this subject, from those who have been more favourably situated for forming a correct judgement. This is a consideration, however, which, though it may disarm the severity of censure, and claim for such individuals the exercise of the utmost candour and charity, does in no degree alter the duty of the British parliament and the British public. If " the existence of slavery," as it now exists in our colonies, be, to use the forcible language of the Edinburgh Reviewer, " an atrocious crime," then " every Englishman who loves his country should dedicate his whole life, and every faculty of his soul, to efface this foul stain from its character," as speedily as is consistent with the safety and well-being of the parties more immediately concerned.

THE

NEGRO SLAVERY *of the* WEST INDIES.

THE main object of the preceding article is stated to have been, " by exhibiting a series of facts, to fix the value of certain general principles which apply to the condition of Negro slavery in all divisions of the civilized world; and to demonstrate that in its leading characteristics, and more prominent tendencies and effects, it is, *when uncontrolled by some powerful external influence* which shall make the emancipation of the slave the ultimate end of its regulations, the same revolting institution, whether it be administered by Spaniards or Portuguese, Frenchmen or Dutchmen, Englishmen or Americans." This is also the main purpose of the present publication. In pursuing it, however, we are anxious to avoid the imputation of unfair dealing towards the holders of slaves in the British colonies. We might have brought forward, in abundance, proofs of the excessive rigour of the slave code in the colonies of the French and Dutch. We might have shown, by an induction of particulars, resting on the best authority, with what terrible ferocity that code is often administered in practice ; how it serves to divest the female character of its most amiable attributes, rendering not the masters only, but the mistresses of slaves, dead alike to the feelings of tenderness and delicacy ; and how it converts even the most sacred functions of criminal justice into the means of indulging the worst passions of the human heart, and of gratifying a barbarous and sanguinary thirst of vengeance. It might be said, however, that, in doing this, we were exciting unjust prejudices against our own West India planters ; that our own colonial institutions bear in themselves a much milder aspect than those of the French and Dutch, and are besides administered by Englishmen, in the spirit, and according to the maxims, of English jurisprudence. We will not now stop to controvert the correctness of this statement ; we will give our countrymen the benefit of the plea, so far at least as to abstain, for the present, from illustrating our general position by facts drawn from the foreign colonies of the West Indies. The proofs already exhibited, in confirmation of it, have been drawn from the nature and effects of the slave system in the United States, the general spirit of whose legislation and jurisprudence is, to say no more, as liberal as our own ; and we mean, in what follows, to confine the examination to the British islands.

Here, again, we propose to take a view of the state of slavery, which must be admitted, by West Indians themselves, to be the least unfavourable to the character of their system. We shall not now have recourse to the writings of that able and faithful delineator of Negro slavery in our own islands, the Rev. James Ramsay ; because the scenes he witnessed, however they may serve to mark the genius of that institution, it might be alleged, are now upwards of forty years old. Neither shall we have recourse to any part of the evidence taken before the Privy Council, or before Parliament, when the question of the Slave Trade was first agitated in this country. We shall not even cite, in support of our general views, the testimony of Dr. Pinckard ; nor the recorded atrocities communicated by Lord Seaforth in 1804, as illustrative of the state of slavery in the oldest of our colonies, Barbadoes ; lest it should be argued, that these authorities do not apply to the actually existing state of things. We shall abstain even from laying any stress on the still more recent exemplifications of the spirit and tendency of colonial slavery, which are furnished to us in the cases of Huggins of Nevis, Hodge of Tortola, and Rawlins of St. Kitts ; lest we should be charged with too much confining our view to small and insulated communities, where individuals are less influenced by public opinion than in larger societies*. We recollect, indeed, to have heard West Indians, when these cases were alluded to in Parliament, challenge the opponents of the slave system to look, for a just appreciation of its character, not to our smaller islands, but to Jamaica, which exceeds them all in extent of population, and the liberal nature of whose institutions they did not hesitate to set up as a model for general imitation. We accept the challenge ; and we propose, therefore, for the present, to confine our view to a consideration of the slave system as it exists in Jamaica, the colony in which we are told that it may be seen under the most favourable circumstances, and where we are also told that the slaves are under the protection of a humane code of laws, humanely and equitably administered.

In this delineation, also, of slavery, as it exists in Jamaica, we shall abstain from selecting particular instances of cruelty, and shall further abstain from specifying such cases of general treatment, in the management of plantations, as might be deemed to be peculiarly harsh and rigorous. On the contrary, we shall select, for our most prominent example, the case of an estate, the owner of which is distinguished even in this country for gentlemanly and kindly feeling; and (which is perhaps of still more importance) is possessed of wealth which relieves him from the necessity, to which many by their circumstances are unhappily driven, of exacting from their slaves an undue portion of labour, or of denying them

---

* Let it not be supposed, that we admit the validity of the objections to which, in the present instance, we think proper to defer. We may have other opportunities of showing that they have no real force whatever.

the requisite supplies for their sustentation and comfort. In short, the proprietor in question, it is well known, is himself an excellent master to his slaves, and does all in his power to render their situation comfortable. But he lives in this country, and is therefore obliged to trust to the agency of others; and in point of fact his best efforts appear to have been employed in vain to mitigate the intrinsic oppressiveness of the system.

The Rev. Thomas Cooper published, in the course of the last year, in a periodical work called The Monthly Repository, several papers, with his name affixed to them, on the subject of Negro Slavery in the West Indies. These papers attracted considerable notice, being evidently the production of an able, intelligent, and upright man; and naturally induced persons taking an interest in the question to communicate with him upon it. The following statement is the result of these communications; and it is now given to the public with the permission of Mr. Cooper himself, who, we are most happy to announce to our readers, is engaged in preparing for the press a more complete detail of his observations on Negro Slavery during his residence in the West Indies, as well as a fuller development of his views on the subject.

I. EVIDENCE OF THE REV. THOMAS COOPER.

In the year 1817, Robert Hibbert, Esq. of East Hide, near Luton, Bedfordshire, engaged the Rev. Thomas Cooper to go over to Jamaica, for the express purpose of ascertaining the practicability of improving, by means of religious instruction, the condition of the Negroes on his estate of Georgia, in the parish of Hanover, in that island. With a view to render his task as agreeable as possible, Mr. Cooper was authorized to adopt his own plans of tuition, " provided they should in no respect be found incompatible with the order and management of the plantation." A house was provided for him, pleasantly situated about a mile from the Negro village, and he was made quite independent of the other White people connected with the slaves. He reached the estate on Christmas day, 1817, and continued upon it for upwards of three years, after which he returned to England, where he now resides.

The owner of this estate, who himself resides in England, is, as may be inferred from his proceedings in this very instance, a man of great benevolence. He was at the entire expense of Mr. Cooper's mission, and he seemed disposed to spare no outlay which he thought likely to contribute to the comfort of his slaves, of whom there were about 400 attached to the estate. The estate had formerly been made to produce 400 hogsheads of sugar; but Mr. Hibbert, considering that the labour required for the production of so large a quantity pressed too heavily upon his slaves, directed that only 300 hogsheads should be made, and it is to this moderated scale of employment, and to a gang of Negroes thus favourably circumstanced, in relation to their proprietor, that Mr. Cooper's information refers.

One great obstacle to his success as a religious instructor, which Mr. Cooper had to encounter at the very outset of his undertaking, was this, that the slaves had no time to attend upon him. This will require a somewhat lengthened explanation, which will serve, at the same time, to throw light incidentally on several material features of the slave system.

The season of crop, in other words, the sugar harvest, commenced about the time of Mr. Cooper's arrival in Jamaica, and continued for about five months. During that period, the general plan is, and that plan was followed on Georgia estate, to begin the manufacture of sugar on Sunday evening, and to continue it generally, without intermission, either day or night, till about midnight of the following Saturday, when the work stops for about eighteen or twenty hours, to commence again on the Sunday evening*. In order to prevent any interruption of this process during the week, the slaves capable of labour, are, with some necessary exceptions, divided into two gangs or spells, which, besides being both fully occupied in the various occupations of the plantation during the day, are engaged the whole of the night, on alternate nights, in the business of sugar making†. Their labour, during crop time, is thus equal to six days and three nights in the week. And in the exaction of this labour, no distinction is made between men and women; both are subjected to the same unvarying rule.

The canes are carried on the backs of mules, or in carts, from

---

* By an act of the Jamaica legislature of Dec. 1816, it is forbidden to set the sugar mills to work before five on Monday morning. But this regulation appears to have been practically disregarded in this instance.

† On many estates the two gangs or spells, instead of alternating the whole of the night, labour half of each night, the one being replaced by the other at midnight.

the field to the mill. The men employed in this part of the work have no regular time of rest, either night or day. Their task is to keep the mill regularly supplied with canes, and it is only when they have been able, by exertion, to accumulate a quantity there, that they can venture to take rest. It seldom happens that they get a whole night's rest at one time. Besides the alternate night of rest allowed to the other slaves, that portion of them who were not attending the sugar works had half an hour allowed them to sit down in the field to eat their breakfast, and two hours further interval of labour allowed them in the middle of the day, generally from one to three. The same allowance of time for breakfast and dinner was continued to the labouring slaves the whole year round *.

During the five months of crop, therefore, it is pretty evident, that it would have been found " incompatible with the order and management of the plantation" to allot any portion of time for religious instruction, unless it were on Sunday.

But here it will be said, that Sunday was the very day on which that instruction might most conveniently and appropriately have been given ; and that it could hardly be alleged, with any fairness, that the Negroes had no time to attend to religious instruction, when the middle of that day might have been set apart for the purpose. To this arrangement, however, Mr. Cooper found there were insuperable objections : it was wholly " incompatible with the order and management of the plantation." In the first place, the persons who had been toiling for six days and three nights in the preceding week, many of whom had continued that toil till past midnight on Saturday, could not be expected voluntarily to assemble, at a very early hour, to listen to lessons which they had not learned to appreciate. In the next place, Sunday was the *only* day which was allowed them, during the five months of crop, for cultivating their provision-grounds ; for bringing thence the food requisite for their sustenance during the week ; and for going to market.

It may not be generally understood, that not only is Sunday a market-day in Jamaica, but that, for the Negroes, whether as venders of the fruit or vegetables or poultry or other articles of food they may have to dispose of, or as purchasers of the little necessa-

* The law referred to above specifies these periods of half an hour and two hours as the proper intervals of labour during the day ; and it adds that, except in crop time, the slaves are not to be obliged to work before five in the morning, or after seven in the evening.

ries or comforts they may wish to buy in return, *Sunday is the only market-day*. Such, however, is the fact.

The distance of the place of market, varying from one to five, ten, and even more miles, and which must be twice traversed by such slaves as go to it, and who have generally heavy loads to carry thither, tends further, independently of the time required for their sales and purchases, to abridge the hours which could, by any possibility, be given to religious worship on the Sunday.

It is some labour even to fetch on that day from their provision-grounds the plantains, or yams, or eddoes, or other food which they may require, to feed themselves and any children they may have, during the succeeding week ; a labour which is often aggravated by the distance of those provision-grounds from the homestall of the plantation,—a distance often extending to six, and sometimes even to ten miles. The distance of the provision-grounds on Georgia estate was about three miles from the Negro village, which was thought moderate. Still the very walk thither and back was sufficient to diminish, by two hours, the brief respite from plantation-labour which Sunday afforded to the slaves.

But besides these different uses to which the Sunday was necessarily appropriated, there remained another of a still more engrossing nature. Sunday was *the only day which was allowed to the slaves, during crop, for cultivating and keeping in order their provision-grounds, from which provision-grounds they derived their sole means of subsistence*, if we except a weekly allowance of seven or eight herrings to each adult, and half that number to each child, and a small present of a pound or two of salt-fish at Christmas. If, therefore, they neglected to employ in their provision-grounds a sufficient portion of the Sunday, to secure to them an adequate supply of food, they might be reduced to absolute want ; and although the want might be supplied, yet the neglect would not fail to be punisned.

When all these circumstances are weighed, we shall have no difficulty in comprehending how it was that Mr. Cooper, during the first five or six months of his residence on Georgia estate, could find no time for the religious instruction of the slaves, which was *compatible with its order and management.*

" The Sunday shone no Sabbath-day to them."

Nor was their case, in this respect, on Mr. Hibbert's estate, at all peculiar. It was the common lot of the plantation slaves generally throughout the island.

Crop-time, however, lasted only for five or at most six months of the year. How did Mr. Cooper succeed during the remaining six or seven months? During those months, as well as during crop-time, the Sunday was wholly and exclusively applied, in the case of the slaves, to the various secular objects already mentioned ; but chiefly and above all, Sunday being the day especially appropriated for the cultivation of their provision-grounds, which were the allotted source of subsistence for themselves and their families while engaged in the weekly labours of the plantation, it was felt to be impossible to require that a portion of it should be given to attendance on religious instruction, at least unless an equivalent portion of time had been given them, during the week, for the purpose of cultivating their grounds. But, even then, to have enforced such attendance on the Sunday would have proved a grievous imposition. It would have operated as an interdict from attending market, on the only day on which there was any market to attend. Under these circumstances, even Mr. Cooper was forced to admit that it would have been the greatest cruelty to compel the slaves to attend Divine worship on Sundays.

But it may be asked whether no time, except Sunday, is given to the slaves for the raising of food. The law of the island requires that one day in a fortnight, except during the time of crop, should be allowed to the slaves, *exclusive of Sunday*, for cultivating their provision-grounds*. This would amount to from fourteen to sixteen days in the year. The proprietor of Georgia was, however, more liberal than the law. There the slaves were allowed for this purpose (and other proprietors in that quarter, Mr. Cooper thinks, may have been equally liberal) every Saturday after crop, until they began to dig the land into holes for the fall-plant, when they were allowed only every second Saturday. By this arrangement, the Negroes belonging to Georgia had about twenty-eight days in the year allowed them for the cultivation of their grounds, besides Sundays.

As this time, however, had been given them for the express pur-

* See the amended Slave Act of Jamaica, presented to the House of Commons, along with various other papers respecting the West Indies, on the 10th June, 1818.

pose of raising their food, it would have been unjust to the slaves, and would have placed both religion and its minister in an odious light, had any part of it been authoritatively diverted from its original destination, with a view to attendance upon him. Accordingly it was agreed that, out of crop, an afternoon every fortnight should be allowed for religious worship and instruction. Mr. Cooper had thus an opportunity of preaching to the slaves about eleven or twelve times in the year. But the moment crop began, there was an entire cessation for five or six months of all meetings of the kind.

After remaining in this unsatisfactory state for upwards of three years, Mr. Cooper, as has been already remarked, quitted Jamaica and returned to Great Britain. He justly observes, that it could perhaps hardly be expected that he should have consented to consume his time amongst a people to whom he could preach only twelve times in the year.

Having thus made our readers in some measure acquainted with the respectable witness to whose testimony we mean in the first instance to refer them, we shall now proceed to adduce his further evidence, both as it respects the particular estate on which he resided, and the condition of the slaves generally in the island. When the statements are general, they are to be considered as comprehending Georgia, unless that estate be particularly excepted.

1. *State of Morals and Religion.*

This, Mr. Cooper states, is as bad as can well be imagined both among Whites and Blacks. With scarcely any exceptions, all of the former description, residing on plantations, live in a state of open and avowed concubinage with Black or Coloured women. The general profligacy, in this respect, is perfectly notorious and undisguised * ; and one effect of it is, that the young women on estates, instead of becoming mothers of children, are at an early age made the mere instruments of licentious gratification. It is well known that the morals of nineteen out of twenty White men are ruined before they have been a month in the island. They get into habits

---

* So undisguised, indeed, is it, that, when visitors stay all night on an estate, they are accustomed, on going to bed, to desire the domestic who attends them to bring them a girl, with almost as little ceremony as they would ask for a candle.

of debauchery, and every idea of religion vanishes. Mr. Cooper does not recollect to have seen a single White man there, who showed any serious concern about religion, excepting some Missionaries.

There is no regular marriage instituted amongst the slaves ; indeed, the women will say they would not be such fools as consent to be confined to one man : their engagements, therefore, are merely temporary, and are not considered as at all binding. Mr. Cooper never heard of any attempt, by agreement between masters, to bring together on the same plantation a man and wife who lived on different plantations. Nor could it in general be of any very great use to do so, while there is no such thing among them as a marriage-tie.

It is, doubtless, in part owing to this cause, and to the universal profligacy of manners prevailing among Blacks and Whites, that the Negroes in Jamaica are a very unprolific race : not that they are so naturally,—but they are made so by the brutalizing and demoralizing system of government under which they live, which is notoriously most unfriendly to the production of life, and, in several ways, tends directly to its destruction. Among other things, it causes the women to be extremely careless of themselves when breeding, so that miscarriages are very common ; and it produces also the most miserable neglect of their children.

The Negroes on Georgia estate do not keep up their numbers. There were in one year only seven births, though the whole population is about four hundred. Mr. Cooper attributes this non-in-increase to their morally degraded condition ; to prostitution and its various consequences, including disease ; to hard work, and to severity of punishment. Indeed, he considers that having no other motive to exertion in their present state, they would not work at all, were it not that neglect would be visited with severe punishment.

In Jamaica the slaves are scarcely ever taught to read.

In every parish there is a rector, who, generally speaking, preaches every Sunday morning at the parish church ; and a curate, who has a chapel. The service, however, takes place at the very time which may be called high-change at the Negro market. Mr. Cooper, when he attended church, may have seen twenty or thirty Negroes there, (whether slaves or free he could not say,) and probably about a dozen Whites. The greater part of the congregation consisted of free Mulattoes. The regular church-service was read, and a sermon preached, which, however, was not at all adapted to the Blacks. It is required by law that there should be service in the afternoon, after market should be over, to suit the time.of Negroes,—when all who might attend should be catechized : but this had not been done in the parish of Hanover ; and he believes not in the adjoining parishes, excepting for a short time at first. It may have dropped in consequence of the non-attendance of the Negroes.

To obviate the complaint that had been made in England of the want of Christian instruction for the slaves, an act was passed instituting a curacy in each parish, expressly for their benefit. The act states that the curates shall appropriate two days in every week to go to some one or other of the estates in rotation, and there to perform the duties of his office, and to instruct all slaves willing to be instructed, *provided the consent of the person in possession of the estate be first obtained.* In consequence of the necessity of obtaining this consent, Mr. Cooper was informed, by the curate of Hanover parish, that he might apply to ten estates before he got leave to preach on one. These applications had a reference only to weekdays ; for it would have been obviously the greatest cruelty to compel the attendance of the slaves at worship on Sunday. Both the rector and curate of Hanover parish said (and the same was true of the adjoining parishes) that they were of no use to the slaves as instructors, and that, under existing circumstances, it was impossible they should. And as for the Curates' Act, it was generally held there to have been passed for the satisfaction of England, and not for any good it was likely to produce.

The character given by Mr. Cooper of the slaves is such as might be expected to be formed by a state of oppression and degradation such as theirs, and in the total absence of all intellectual, or moral and religious culture. He represents them as addicted to thieving ; but he adds, that to this vice, in some cases, they are strongly tempted, by the unreasonable conduct of the planters themselves. These generally refuse to sell any of their sugar in the island ; the consequence is, that those who are not sugar-planters can procure it only in a concealed and smuggled way, in the Negro market, where it is all stolen sugar. Mr. Cooper, who refused to buy any such, was obliged to tell the attorney of Georgia, that if he would not allow him to have some sugar on the estate, he must send to London for it.

The following passage we give entire. It is taken from a letter of Mr. Cooper's in the Monthly Repository of 1822, p. 494.

" Liberty seems evidently to be the natural right of every human being. Why not then admit of their being prepared for the enjoyment of privileges which cannot be held from them without acting contrary to the sacred laws of truth and justice? The planters, however, are not the only persons with whom I would remonstrate upon this subject; for all who indulge in the consumption of West India produce, or contribute in any way to the maintenance of the present order of things in our sugar-islands, ought in common fairness to bear their share of the blame. With what propriety can a consumer of *rum* or *sugar* cast a stone at the *cultivator* of the sweet cane? The Negro is the injured individual; he is robbed of his liberty, and, with that, of every thing that can render a rational existence desirable. He is denied all the advantages of education, condemned to the vilest ignorance, lest, by becoming informed, he should discover and seek to remove the cause of all his unmerited misfortunes. He cannot marry, and is thereby not merely tempted, but in a manner compelled, to form the loosest and most disgusting connections. I would appeal to the common discernment and feelings of mankind, whether marriage can exist where a *third* person has it in his power to step in and disannul the holy league. Now, every one knows that this is virtually the case with respect to the slaves in the West Indies. The connections which they form do not always take place between individuals belonging to the same proprietor; in numerous instances they are the property of different masters. But it is no uncommon thing for the inhabitants of one plantation or settlement to be removed to another, situated perhaps on the opposite side of the island; and consequently, in all such cases, husbands, wives, and children, belonging to other gangs, are, contrary no doubt to the wishes of the respective masters, left behind. Others again are seized, and sold to pay the debts of their owners. These evils might be removed by attaching them to the soil, but then others would remain of a nature almost equally formidable. Every slave being compelled, under pain of corporal punishment, to yield implicit obedience to the will of the master, the wife as well as the husband would be under the necessity of joining a gang under the command of a driver, and, in case of not giving him satisfaction, to submit to the most degrading chastisement administered in the most indecent manner. I have known them point to things of this description, for the purpose of showing that it is impossible for them to marry. Over their children it is obvious that they could have no authority resembling that which parents in a free country possess : they could only leave them the same wretched inheritance which they received from their ancestors. Hence those who have children are generally careless in respect to the habits they form, and the lives they lead. They know they can never sink lower in the scale of society than they already find themselves placed, and they have no hope of rising. A regular line of orderly conduct may save them from the lash, but it can effect no radical change in their condition. The highest office to which they can ever aspire is that of a driver,—an office which no one, not destitute of every manly and generous feeling, could wish to hold. In short, they have nothing to gain and nothing to lose ; they have no character at stake ; a good name, which Solomon says, ' is rather to be chosen than great riches,' is of no avail to them. Their worth is estimated by the strength of their bodies, and the talent and disposition to perform their masters' work. The greatest villain, therefore, in a moral respect, may be, and sometimes is, the most valuable slave; the natural consequence of all which is, that the Negroes, as a people, are as destitute of correct morality as they are of liberty. Chastity is utterly out of the question amongst the whole tribe, and both men and women are found to vindicate as innocent, practices which it is scarcely allowable to name amongst Christians. This is followed by low cunning and contempt of truth, a determined resolution to thieve, and the greatest aversion to every species of labour. Gratitude, affection, fidelity, activity, and courage, make no part of the character of the West India slave; and yet thousands and tens of thousands have been ' received into the congregation of Christ's flock, and signed with the sign of the cross,' &c. &c. I have been present, more than once, at the christening of two or three hundred of them, and repeatedly conversed with persons who have been *thus* regenerated. Need I add that the whole is a solemn mockery of what the people are exhorted to regard as a Christian rite ? No effort whatever that I could ever learn is made to prepare them for the ceremony, or, after it is performed, to enforce its design. The poor creatures get a new name, with which they are mightily pleased, and some of them are said to fancy themselves out of the reach of Obeah or witchcraft. Within the last few years, it is true, curates have been sent out for the avowed purpose of instructing them in religion; but, it is to be feared, they meet with no adequate success. The Negroes cannot attend on their service on a Sunday; and when I left Jamaica no regulations had been made, or I believe thought of, for allowing them time in the week. These Missionaries are expected to visit several estates every week, for the purpose of preaching to the slaves, if they can obtain leave of the proprietor, or person acting in his place, to do so. But this they very seldom get; on some estates not at all, on others once or twice in the year; so that their presence in the island can be of little importance. I have heard it, indeed, repeatedly declared that the Curates' Act was intended for England, not for Jamaica; and this really appears to me to be viewing the subject in its true light; for it must have been known, before it was passed, that the planters would not allow the slaves any opportunity for attending on their new instructors, and that, consequently, such a law could have no tendency to improve their condition. In a thousand instances the clergy are rather to be pitied than blamed; and I have not the least doubt that many a curate most deeply laments that ever he crossed the Atlantic."

In a subsequent letter Mr. Cooper observes, that if a man would but " fix on his mind a clear picture of *a master treading on his slave with the feet of despotism,* he would perceive the cruel mockery of the same individual pretending, while in such an attitude, to raise his wretched victim with the hand of mercy." There is, he affirms, among slave-holders generally, " the strongest prejudice to any thing which is in any way calculated to open the minds of their people."—" Ignorance, gross ignorance," is conceived to be " the grand prop of Negro slavery." Nay, he believes it to be the common opinion in Jamaica, " that the Negroes are an inferior species."

2. *General Treatment.*

The gangs always work before the whip, which is a very weighty and powerful instrument. The driver has it always in his hand,

and drives the Negroes, men and women without distinction, as he would drive horses or cattle in a team. Mr. Cooper does not say that he is always using the whip, but it is known to be always present, and ready to be applied to the back or shoulders of any who flag at their work, or lag behind in the line*. The driver, who is generally a Black man, has the power not only of thus stimulating the slaves under him to exertion, by the application of the whip to their bodies while they are proceeding with their work ; but, when he considers any of them to have committed a fault deserving of a more serious notice, he has the power also of prostrating them (women as well as men) on the ground, causing them to be held firmly down by other Negroes, who grasp the hands and legs of their prostrate companion, when he may inflict upon the bare posteriors such a number of lashes as he may deem the fault to have merited ; the whole number which he may inflict at one time, without the presence of the overseer, being, by the Slave Act of 1816, limited to ten. One of the faults which the driver most frequently punishes in this way, is that of coming too late to the field either in the morning or after dinner. Those who arrive after the fixed time are pretty sure to get a few, perhaps five or six lashes. Mr. Cooper, on one occasion, saw three or four old women come too late ; they knew they were to be whipped, and as soon as they came up threw themselves down on the ground to receive the lashes ; some of them received four, others six lashes. These minor punishments, Mr. Cooper says, are very frequent. He believes that seldom a day passes without some occurring ; and he has heard of as many as sixty Negroes being flogged in one morning for being late.

More serious punishments are only inflicted by the authority of the overseer ; and the mode of their infliction is usually the same as has been already described. Whether the offender be male or female, precisely the same course is pursued. The posteriors are made bare, and the offender is extended prone on the ground, the hands and feet being firmly held and extended by other slaves ; when the driver, with his long and heavy whip, inflicts, under the

* In one of his printed letters, in which he is replying to an objection, Mr. Cooper incidentally but very significantly remarks, that " to a Jamaica man" it would be truly astonishing " to learn that the whip was not needed, or that its sound was rarely heard."

eye of the overseer, the number of lashes which he may order; each lash, when the skin is tender and not rendered callous by repeated punishments, making an incision on the buttocks, and thirty or forty such lashes leaving them in a dreadfully lacerated and bleeding state. Even those that have become the most callous cannot long resist the force of this terrible instrument, when applied by a skilful hand, but become also raw and bloody; indeed, no strength of skin can withstand its reiterated application.

These punishments are inflicted by the overseer whenever he thinks them to have been deserved. He has no written rules to guide his conduct, nor are the occasions at all defined on which he may exercise the power of punishment. Its exercise is regulated wholly and solely by his own discretion. An act of neglect or of disobedience, or even a look or a word supposed to imply insolence, no less than desertion or theft or contumacy, may be thus punished; and they may be thus punished without trial and without appeal, at the mere pleasure and fiat of the overseer. Doubtless, any slave may, *after having been punished*, complain of his overseer to the attorney of the estate, or to a magistrate; but such complaint often does him more harm than good.

The law professes to limit the number of lashes, which shall be given at one time to thirty-nine; but neither this law, nor any other which professes to protect the slave, can be of much practical benefit to him; it cannot, under existing circumstances, be enforced, and its existence in the statute book therefore is but a mockery. A Negro, especially one who is the slave of an absentee proprietor, may be considered as entirely in the power of the overseer, who is his absolute master, and may be at the same instant his lawgiver, accuser, and judge, and may not only award sentence, but order its execution. And supposing him to act unjustly, or even cruelly he has it in his power to prevent any redress from the law. The evidence of a thousand slaves would avail nothing to his conviction; and, even if there were any disposition in the inferior Whites to inform or to bear testimony against him, he has only to take care that the infliction does not take place in their presence.

In point of fact, Mr. Cooper believes that the limitation of the number of lashes to thirty-nine is practically disregarded, whenever the overseer thinks the offence deserving of a larger measure of punishment. The information he received on this subject all went to show that the law was not attended to. One overseer told him, that a woman had disobeyed his orders, and he put her in the stocks by way of punishment. She complained to the attorney of this proceeding. He ordered her to be thrown down on the ground, in the customary manner, and thirty-nine lashes were inflicted on her naked posteriors; after which she was raised up, and immediately thrown down again, and received thirty-nine lashes more, applied in the same manner.

The law permits the Negroes to make their complaints to magistrates. In one case several Negroes went to complain to a magistrate of their want of houses, or proper accommodation. Mr. Cooper saw them, on that occasion, at the magistrate's door. The magistrate, however, told him it would never do to interfere in such matters; for, if they did, there would be no getting on between masters or overseers, and magistrates; and, with respect to these complainants, what he did was to desire them to return home and trust to their master's kindness: and Mr. Cooper thought that, all things considered, he could not well have done otherwise.

Two women, who were pregnant, desired to quit the field during rain, on account of their pregnancy. The overseer refused them permission. They went to complain of this refusal to a magistrate, but were stopped in their way by a neighbouring overseer, and by him thrown into the stocks until he sent them back to their own overseer, who put them again into the stocks on their own estate, and had them flogged. Of this proceeding they complained to the attorney. The attorney was of opinion that the overseer had acted with undue severity; but he considered the women to have been highly to blame for attempting to complain to the magistrate; whereas, he said, they ought in the first instance to have complained to him.

It is common for Negroes, who have been guilty of what is deemed a serious offence, to be worked all day in the field, and during the intervals of labour, as well as during the whole night, to be confined with their feet fast in the stocks. In the case of one Negro, who was so confined for some weeks, Mrs. Cooper begged hard to obtain a remission of his punishment, but did not succeed. Another Negro, belonging to the estate, was a notorious runaway. Being taken, he was flogged in the usual manner, as severely as he well could bear, and then made to work in the field. During the interval of dinner-time he was regularly placed in the

E

stocks, and in them also he was confined the whole night. When he lacerations, produced by the flogging he had received, were sufficiently healed, he was flogged a second time. While the sores were still unhealed, one of the book-keepers told Mr. Cooper that maggots had bred in the lacerated flesh. Mr. Cooper mentioned the circumstance to the attorney, who did not manifest any surprise on hearing it.

An old African Negro, well known to Mr. Cooper, who appeared to possess a sound and superior mind, and was reckoned the best watchman on the estate, was placed to watch the provision-grounds for the use of the overseer's house. These were robbed, and the robbery being imputed to his neglect, he received a very severe flogging. The old man declared (Mr. Cooper does not vouch for the truth of the excuse) that he could not help what had happened, the grounds being too extensive for him to guard them effectually, so that while he was on one side of them, the Negroes could easily steal on the other. This flogging made a great alteration in the old man, and he never seemed well after it. In two or three weeks another robbery occurring, he received a still more severe flogging than before. One morning, while Mr. and Mrs. Cooper were at breakfast, they heard a groaning, and going to the window, saw this poor man passing along in a state which made Mrs. Cooper shrink back with horror. Mr. Cooper went out to him, and found his posteriors, which were completely exposed, much lacerated, and bleeding dreadfully. He seemed much exhausted. He attempted to explain the case, but was incapable from fatigue and suffering. A Negro boy was standing by; the old man pointed to him, and said, " Massa, him tell you." The poor old man from this time was never well or cheerful, and he soon afterwards died.

Mr. Cooper never saw a Negro, who, when uncovered, did not exhibit marks of violence, that is to say, traces of the whip, on his body.

It has been already mentioned that the Negroes on this estate, and the same is the case generally throughout the island, have no food beyond a small allowance of salted fish, except what they raise on their own grounds; Sundays, and a certain number of days beside, being allotted for their cultivation.

The Negroes have in general too few houses; but the having a house to themselves, be it ever so bad, gives some feeling of importance. On Georgia there are many houses built in rather a superior style, which have cost the proprietor a heavy sum of money; but in general their huts are like sheds. They are made with posts put into the ground. The sides are wattled, some being plastered with mortar, and some not. They are thatched, sometimes shingled. They often have one room to sit in, with one or two for sleeping. They lie on boards, or on a door covered with a mat of their own making, and sometimes a blanket for covering; but they have not all blankets. A woman with children has a blanket, and also the aged men; but many men have none.

3. *Emancipation.*

If the mother be three degrees removed from the Black, her child by a White man is free, and classes, in point of privilege, with Whites.

White men occasionally give freedom to their mistresses and their children. But this, in all cases where the mistress and her children are not the slaves of the White man, must be effected by purchase, and, of course, with the owner's consent. But such purchases cannot be effected when the estate is mortgaged, or the owner is a minor. White men often complain that the owner is not compelled to give freedom to their children, on his being paid their value. In all cases where slaves are made free, a bond must be given that they shall not become chargeable.

Free Blacks and persons of Colour pay all taxes, and perform military duty in the colonial militia, precisely as the Whites. According to the number of Negroes which each planter possesses, he is obliged to have upon his estate a certain number of White persons, or to pay a certain sum for each deficiency. This is with a view to prevent the militia from falling off in numbers. Free people of Colour, though they are bound to serve in the militia, yet are of no avail in freeing any estate on which they may be employed from this penalty. Indeed, from the prejudice existing against them in the minds of the Whites, it is in very few cases that they are employed on estates, which, considering the perfect competency of many of them, they feel to be a great hardship. So far indeed are they from being encouraged in Jamaica, that their increase is viewed with apprehension, as adding to the danger of insurrection. Much jealousy is entertained of them, especially when they have been educated in England, where they have been treated as men, and on a footing of equality with their White brethren. And yet Mr. Cooper is of opinion, and in that opinion we entirely concur, that "the principle of gradual emancipation," though the subject of so much alarm to West Indians, affords the best means of remedying the evils of the system, with safety to the master and the slave.

It is a strong proof of the degrading light in which free persons of Colour are viewed by the Whites, that these last never introduce even their own children into company. It was thought a very extraordinary thing, on one occasion, to see a father riding in a gig with his own Coloured daughter. Coloured persons reputed to be children of the owners of the estates are sometimes held as slaves upon them, and have been even sold along with them.

Many of the free Negroes are industrious, and succeed very well, although they never think of hiring themselves to the planters to work in the field. It could not indeed be expected that they should submit to the degradation of working under the lash. They are objects of great respect to the slaves, but are kept at a distance by the free Browns, who consider themselves as rising in rank as they approach to the colour of Whites.

Very great difficulty is experienced by Negroes in obtaining their freedom, even when they are able to pay for it; because those who by their industry and frugality have realized the means of purchasing their freedom, and who, therefore, are most worthy of it, and also likely to employ it most beneficially, are the most valuable hands. Mr. Cooper knew three valuable men who wished to purchase their freedom. They had long applied in vain to the agents of the proprietor resident on the spot. They at length, however, obtained their end, by an application to the proprietor himself, then in England. After this a fourth made many efforts to obtain his freedom by purchase; but they proved unavailing, and he sunk in consequence into a state of despondency, and became of comparatively little value.

The number of Brown slaves, the children of White men, is very considerable. In general, however, they are not employed in the field: Mr. Cooper knew only one estate on which Brown slaves were so employed, viz. Roundhill in Hanover. They are usually employed as domestics, or taught mechanic arts, as carpenters, coopers, masons, smiths, &c.

4. *Miscellaneous Observations.*

A large proportion of all the estates are mortgaged; and estates are frequently sold to pay off the debts upon them. The slaves themselves, too, or a part of them, are often seized for the payment of the master's debts; and this is done without any reference, in a multitude of cases, to family connections. It is felt by them as a grievous hardship to be separated from their connections: it sometimes produces a species of rebellion; and has been known to occasion the death of many, through the distress of mind which it produces.

Small proprietors often undertake to do work on estates by job, which they employ their slaves to execute. When they are thus sent to different places, they carry their own provisions with them, and usually sleep on the ground under a tent, all huddled together though sometimes they are accommodated in the sugar-works of the estate, or by the Negroes of the estate in their houses.

Task-work is very uncommon in Jamaica. It is held to be dangerous to allow the slave much spare time.

If a Negro is deemed to be incorrigible by plantation-discipline, he is often sent to the workhouse of the parish, where he is chained to another Negro, and employed, with others chained in the same manner, two and two, in repairing the roads during the day, being shut up during the night. This punishment is inflicted without the intervention of any magistrate, by the mere desire of the master or overseer, who may protract it for any length of time.

When Negroes are sent out in pursuit of runaways, they are usually armed with a cutlass, and are authorized, in case of resistance, to chop, that is, to cut down the runaway. The Maroons are also encouraged by rewards to take up runaways. They carry firearms, and may shoot them if they resist.

There is on every estate what the Negroes call a Hothouse or Hospital, which a medical practitioner is expected to visit once or twice a week. The Negroes have generally a great dislike to being shut up in this Hothouse, where they are separated from the kindness of their friends, and would prefer being in their own houses, even though in a miserable state.

White women, who are owners of slaves, will, in general, without any scruple, order their slaves to be flogged, and some of them will even stand by to see them stripped bare, and punished in the usual disgusting manner.

Just before Mr. Cooper quitted the island, as he was walking in the streets of Lucea, the port-town of Hanover parish, in company with the captain of the vessel in which he had taken his passage, they saw an old man who appeared to have been recently flogged. He was standing in the public street with his posteriors exposed and bleeding, and yet he seemed to excite no attention whatever from any one but Mr. Cooper and the captain.

Such is the unbiassed testimony of this respectable Christian minister on the subject of Negro slavery, as it exists at the present time in our island of Jamaica. The statements he has made do not consist of instances of cruelty collected in a long series of years, or from different parts of the island; but they refer to one neighbourhood, and mostly to one estate; and that estate, too, not singled out for the harshness or inhumanity of its treatment, but such an estate as would be as likely as any other to have been selected in order to convey the most favourable representation of Negro bondage; being an estate the owner of which is conspicuous for his benevolence, and seems sincerely desirous of sparing no expense to make his slaves as comfortable as circumstances will allow. Do not these facts, therefore, furnish a strong presumption, we will not say against the owners of slaves, but against the system which they administer, as incurably vicious, unless the British Parliament shall interfere to apply a remedy adequate to the occasion, by paving the way for a gradual emancipation, and in the mean time by abating the evils which will otherwise be found to be inseparable from that degrading and disgusting state of society which exists in our West India islands?

The valuable statements of Mr. Cooper appear to us to possess this great recommendation, that they are given (as may be more clearly seen by a perusal of his papers in the Monthly Repository) with an admirable dispassionateness, and without the slightest feeling of irritation towards the planters, whether proprietors or overseers. On the contrary, with a candour that does him the highest honour, he becomes, in some respects, their apologist, attributing the evils which he specifies and deplores, mainly to the system they are called to adminster, rather than to any particular disposition, on their part, to administer it oppressively, or to abuse the tremendous power they possess. He conceives them to be forced, by circumstances, " to continue to whip on their unwilling gangs, as a postboy does his hacks from mile to mile." What an idea does this single sentence convey of the nature of Negro slavery !

But, after all that can be said in favour of the slave-holders is admitted, we would ask, Is it possible to expect that such power as theirs should not be abused ? Or that the men who possess it, and who are stated to have cast off the fear of God, and to experience little or no controul from human laws, should not be tyrannical, capricious, and cruel ? To suppose this, would be to suppose the planters of Jamaica to be angels and not men.

II. EVIDENCE OF JOHN WILLIAMSON, M.D.

In the year 1817 Dr. Williamson published a work, in two volumes 8vo, entitled " Medical and Miscellaneous Observations relative to the West India Islands*, by John Williamson, M.D. Fellow of the Royal College of Physicians, Edinburgh, formerly Surgeon of the Caithness Highlanders, and late of Spanish Town, Jamaica." He dedicates this work to the Earl of Harewood, on whose estate of Williamsfield, in the parish of St. Thomas in the Vale, Jamaica, he had lived for about four years in a professional capacity†. His residence in the island appears to have extended from August 1798 to April 1812, a period of nearly fourteen years.

The testimony of Dr. Williamson will be less liable to exception, in the estimation of West Indians, as he shows himself, on all occasions, a sturdy advocate of their system ; and when he finds fault with them, it is manifestly with extreme reluctance. He even hopes, by an exhibition of facts, to place in their true light the unfair representations of the enemies of the colonies, " the officious would-be friends" (as he calls them) " of humanity," who, he assures us, have only to " leave the Negroes to their own judgement, and to improvement by the wisely framed resolutions of their own

* See an able review of this work in the Edinburgh Review, vol. xxviii. p. 340.

† On this estate Dr. Williamson states, that every thing was conducted on principles of liberality highly honourable to his lordship. He resided there free of expense, and every comfort was afforded him he could have wished for. Vol. i. p. 76.

colonial assemblies," in order to their being "a happy people," who will "fully appreciate the value of their superior condition." Vol. i. p. 338.—He sometimes expresses himself in terms almost approaching to rapture, when speaking of the condition of the Negroes in the West Indies; nay, he even doubts whether the abolition of the slave trade was not a great evil, inasmuch as it prevented the removal of Africans from a state of barbarism and misery, in their own land, to that state of civilization and improvement, a West Indian plantation! (Vol. i. p. 371. ii. p. 332, &c. &c.)

One of the blessings attending this removal he rather amusingly discovers to be, that "indolent, good-for-nothing Negroes," (and it seems there are many of these in Jamaica,) who, "if they were left to their own free wills, uncontrolled by *wholesome laws* which encourage industrious habits, would become idlers and plunderers, and return to barbarism," (vol. i. p. 345.) here find the control of *such wholesome laws.* In other words, their indolence finds a cure, and their industry an incentive *in the wholesome discipline of the cart-whip.* In short, whenever Dr. W. speaks in *general* terms, he seems at a loss to find words strong enough in which to eulogize the humanity and tenderness of West India proprietors and overseers. But let us come to particulars, in order to see how far his facts tend to contradict or to corroborate his panegyric; and, that this may be better understood, we shall range our extracts from this work under the same general heads which we adopted in the case of Mr. Cooper's information.

1. *State of Morals and Religion.*

" The manner in which Sunday is spent," observes Dr. W., " will appear extraordinary, and very contradictory to the duties inculcated on that day. A great market is kept by the Negroes, which is, in truth, also a market for the Whites. The merchants attend at their stores and counting-houses." (vol. i. p. 42.)

" The sacred observance of Sunday appears to me," he says, " necessary, if we expect any good effect from the commands of God. In countries where the duties of that day are becomingly attended to, a greater proportion of virtue, &c. is to be observed. On the contrary, where the Sabbath is violated, the manners of the mass of the people are vicious, regardless of every commendable principle, and afford examples of human depravity which, it is with reluctance I must say, is too applicable to that country (Jamaica). It is much to be wished, that the fourth commandment were more fully taken into consideration. It seems *possible* to do away *Sunday markets*, and *cultivating the ground. Sugar-mills should not be at work on that day,* indeed no labour allowed. It was appointed, by Divine authority, to be a day of rest and devotion, in which no work should be performed." (Vol. i. p. 108.)

" It must be admitted," he goes on to remark, " that the means of religious instruction to Negroes, in Jamaica, are yet extremely defective; and, it is still more painful to add, that the White inhabitants are culpably inattentive to public religious duties. It were well if that were all. *Contempt for religion is openly avowed by a great proportion of those to be met with in that country."* (Vol. i. p. 328.)

" The propriety of matrimony," he tells us, " is seldom impressed on the minds of the Negroes, by the clergy or any other White persons. Indeed, the latter, themselves, show the example of a libidinous course of life, and follow that promiscuous intercourse which can scarcely be justified in savages." (Vol. i. p. 329.)

" At our parish-church, the people of Colour behaved themselves with the greatest propriety, but the White persons conducted themselves with great indecency."—" It is impossible, however, to do any thing," (in the way of religious improvement,) " unless a becoming observance of the Sabbath is enforced. At present, it is a day of *labour, marketing,* and *exchange,* and too often is concluded by *scenes of excess and brutal debauchery. That system is authorized by the Whites.* But until done away, and that, as an introduction to Christian habits among the Negroes, nothing can be so futile as to attempt to reconcile Christianity with a violation of one of its most important commandments." (Vol. i. p. 331.)

" Such a state of things among a people arrogating to themselves the designation of Christians," he adds, " is of a nature so criminal, that to that we may ascribe the destructive line of conduct followed by the Negroes, affecting their lives and health, and the ultimate interests of those who are the cause of these evils."—" No circumstance is, in my opinion, so adverse to the prevalence of Christianity among Negroes as the conduct of the White inhabitants, who treat the Sabbath with a violation of its most sacred duties, and make it, by the *established customs of the island,* a day of *marketing, labour, dancing,* and *excesses of every kind.*" (Vol. ii. p. 285.)

Sunday, Dr. W. conceives, is the only day on which instruction can be conveniently given. But " on that day the Negroes," he tells us, " are engaged in *marketing* and *labour.* They are thus taught to disobey the command which enjoins the observance of the Sabbath ; and it is impossible to suppose that a consistent impression can be made on the minds of Negroes, where the slightest sagacity on their part must expose the absurdity. While the legislature of Jamaica does not provide that Sunday shall be a day of rest, and enforce attention to it, I cannot persuade myself to believe their sincerity." (Vol. ii. p. 287.)

Let us hear Dr. Williamson's testimony respecting another class of evils :—" A stranger is much surprised to observe the domestic attachments which many of the most respectable of the White inhabitants form with females of Colour."—" Among the Negroes, licentious appetites are promiscuously gratified ; and the truth requires that it should not be concealed, the Whites on estates follow the same habits, on many occasions, to a greater extent. Black or Brown mistresses are considered necessary appendages to every establishmen : even a young bookkeeper, coming from Europe, is generally instructed to provide himself ; and however repugnant may seem the idea at first, his scruples are overcome, and he conforms to general custom." Vol. i. pp. 42. 49.)

Dr. Williamson, after enumerating a variety of causes of disease to which the circumstances of the Negroes expose them, adds, " Feelings of humanity and interest concur to deplore that condition of moral turpitude which has proved the source of so many evils to that devoted country."—" That unrestrained habit of promiscuous intercourse, which almost universally prevails in Jamaica, is, in itself, an insuperable bar to population."—" Negro women, in that unrestrained and corrupt line of conduct they are apt to pursue, on arriving at puberty, contract habits inimical to all decency, and particularly adverse to all probability of increasing numbers on the estate." He then proposes a plan for placing them under discreet superintendence, until married to persons of their own colour ; and adds, somewhat obscurely, but with a dreadful significancy, " Such a course would preclude that barbarous and violent line of conduct adopted on such occasions." * (Vol. ii. pp. 131. 199.)

From these, and similar causes, " the diseases of pregnancy," Dr. W. thinks, " are aggravated in Negro women. Abortion is so frequent as to lead to an opinion, that means are taken to procure it, *on account of ill disposition† to their masters, and other barbarous reasons, for which there can be no excuse."*—" Unless means are adopted to bring the women to civilized habits, it will undoubtedly follow that every year will discover a prodigious decrease in our Negro population." (Vol. ii. pp. 199, 200.)

" An *unlucky*" (what a singular epithet to employ on the occasion !) " an unlucky habit of debasement has established itself, by long custom on estates, of bookkeepers attaching themselves to mistresses, slaves on the estate," &c. (Vol. ii. p. 252.)

But enough of this.

2. *General Treatment.*

" An imperfect, confused manner is adopted in Jamaica," Dr. Williamson informs us, " for providing suitably for sick Negroes in the Hothouse, or Hospital."

" The *utmost*" he can say in their favour is, " that in *extreme cases*, where *danger* is represented, the most humane attentions are in general rendered, and nothing wanting which can conduce to comfort or recovery."—Chronic diseases, and lues, he says, are little attended to ; and though it would be for the interest of the proprietors, and of humanity, if they were attended to, yet " any attempts at innovation are resisted."

" If the practitioner were earnestly disposed to insist on his prescriptions and other instructions being obeyed, he would find his best efforts ineffectual ; and it would be better, on the whole,

---

* This sentence furnishes one of the many instances which occur in Dr. Williamson's book, of reluctant admissions, or dark intimations of evils, the combined result of profligacy and hard-heartedness (lust and cruelty) in persons armed with power, which, however intelligible they may be to his West Indian friends, can convey no very clear ideas to persons used only to the decencies and restraints of European society.

† One perceives, in such expressions as these, the influence of colonial society, even on a mind so humane and considerate as Dr. Williamson's. Thus, on another occasion, he tells us that the wretched slaves, who commit suicide, do so from being ill disposed to their masters. (Vol. i. p. 95.)

by cultivating friendship with the overseer, to promote that object." In short, he confesses that "the nature of medical practice was unsatisfactory on estates and plantations." He complains of overseers dismissing patients from the Hospital, in opposition to the advice of the medical attendant; thus accounting for the many instances of irrecoverable venereal cases. The liberal and humane intentions of proprietors*, he further complains, are not carried, into effect. He has had often to lament that his own well-considered prescriptions to subdue a chronic disease, and to restore an additional healthy labourer to his employer, were *completely frustrated* by the negligence of overseers." Dr. Williamson, in another place, specifies an instance where, in attempting the cure of a chronic complaint, which was proceeding favourably, " the unfortunate man was turned out to work by the overseer ; and, though he might labour for a while, would most probably become a victim to incurable disease." (Vol. i. pp. 55. 63. 65. 185.)

" The Yawy Negroes," he further observes, " on estates, seemed to me to be in a very neglected state. In the progress of disease, *that maintenance was not afforded them* which, with a view to cure, should be liberally dispensed. A disease, itself injurious to the constitution, is thus aggravated; whereas, if nature were supported by *fit diet, clothing, cleanliness, and comfortable housing,* she would work her own cure in most cases. An immense deal of labour is thus lost to the proprietor. But this is not all ; for, owing to patched up cures, there is a premature disappearance of the Yawy eruption, and the disease lies lurking in the system ; bone-aches attack the unfortunate Negro ; the master loses a valuable servant ; and the servant drags on a miserable existence."— " The legislature has not interfered in this important matter." (Vol. i. p. 88.)

" The great mortality among infants, the first two weeks after birth," ought, he says, to have secured " the notice of all engaged in plantation-interests, from the proprietor downwards." In St. Thomas in the Vale, " the loss of infants was great beyond what could be imagined." On inquiry, *the bad management* accounted to him for the *mortality.* (Vol. i. p. 130.)

---

* It was while residing on the estate of the Earl of Harewood that Dr. Williamson penned these remarks; and though the remarks themselves are strong, yet how much more strong are the implications which they convey!

" At Newhall estate, where the Negroes were indulged, and considered of dissipated habits, a great deal of bad health occurred."

" The hospitals on estates are much in want of hot and cold baths, which might be erected at a moderate expense. A plan had been given in some time before for that purpose; and the liberal proprietor of Newhall had directed his overseer to have it done: but his orders were not obeyed." (P. 155.)

" It is painful for me to remark," observes the Doctor on another occasion, " that on an estate, a valuable Negro was prevented, by the commands of an overseer, from availing himself of medical prescriptions, while labouring under a pulmonic complaint. My opinion was given to the overseer, with a prescription. Several weeks after, the Negro met me. An increased illness was expressed by his general appearance, and he declared he had neither received medicine nor indulgence, as I had directed. The consequences were, in a short time, fatal to a decent Negro, whose overseer could not deny him to have been a dutiful servant, and respectable in his station.*

On another estate, " a woman, for a trivial offence, was confined in the stocks, in a cold room, night and day, and her life endangered by neglect." Again, " A pregnant woman was confined to the stocks for misconduct, and only liberated a few days before her delivery. Her health had suffered severely, and, after bringing a child, she discovered symptoms of puerperal fever, which terminated her existence in a few days." (Vol. i. p. 191.)

Negroes are represented by Dr. Williamson as " very liable to affections of the mind, which produce diseases of various kinds." Among these Dr. Williamson reckons the *mal d'estomac*, or dirt-eating, which " when it has once established itself among a gang of Negroes, we cannot possibly calculate on the extent of its ravages. It has been observed, however," he adds, " that *on estates where the Negroes are extremely comfortable, this disease is seldom, if ever, discovered.*" (Vol. ii. p. 261.)

The professional pursuits of Dr. Williamson have, naturally enough, led his thoughts chiefly to the *medical* treatment of the

---

* He speaks of another case of a female, where he promised himself success in the treatment: but he says, " The overseer wanted labour; and in these circumstances we must not attempt to thwart the overseer." (Vol. i. p. 249.)

Negroes. It is to this point that his observations are principally
directed. Still, much incidentally breaks out, which throws light
on the prevailing spirit and tendency of the colonial system, as it
affects the well-being of the slaves. Some of the following extracts, however, from Dr. Williamson's work, have a more general
bearing :—

" The overseer of an estate indulged a disposition to amorous
connection with a handsome Negro woman, the adopted wife of a
Negro cooper, with whom she had lived as such for some time.
She was the mother of children to her husband, and they lived
together in a comfortable way. The woman declared herself unwilling to indulge the overseer in a wish so injurious to her husband's happiness ; but *his orders were to be obeyed*, and she
yielded to his desires ; and he aggravated the act by insisting that
she should altogether live with him. It is painful to me to be
obliged to add, that the woman's husband became the object of his
resentment. He was annoyed for having expressed discontent at
such an invasion of his happiness. His life became a burden ; and
though his wife was the companion of the overseer's bed, plots for
his destruction were contemplated by the woman and her injured
husband." Arsenic was mixed in lemonade for the overseer. He
perceived the metallic taste, and did not drink of it ; but a book-
keeper took a draught of it, which produced uneasy sensations ;
but a brisk emetic being administered, prevented fatal consequences. After an inquiry, " it was pretty clearly ascertained,
that the Negro woman, seduced from her husband, had mixed the
dose," hoping that the overseer would have been " the just object
of vengeance, by forfeiting his life." (Vol. i. p. 374.)

Dr. Williamson proceeds no further with the story. He does
not inform us what became either of the Negroes or of the overseer. It was due to the character of the country to have stated
this. In a subsequent part of his work, (vol. ii. p. 201.) he again
briefly adverts to the occurrence, but without attempting to satisfy
our curiosity as to the fate of the parties concerned. He founds on
it indeed a salutary monition to Whites, against pursuing the gratification of their licentious appetites, by the exercise of authority ;
and states it as his opinion that nothing operates more injuriously
on the comfort of the Negro women than such cruel invasions of
their domestic enjoyments. (Vol. ii. p. 201.)

Dr. Williamson remarks, " that where corporal punishment is least exercised, that property is always under the best management." And he recommends that, in all cases of punishment, " the Negro's name, his crime, the extent of punishment and of confinement, should be regularly entered in a book, and that no overseer, or person under his authority, should inflict any punishment which should not thus be brought within notice, or punish a Negro in any shape, but in the presence of a White man belonging to the estate,* whose name must be entered in the book; the whole to be sworn to by the overseer." (Vol. i. p. 193.)

He afterwards recurs to this subject, and is so impressed with the injurious nature of the punishments which it is in the power of overseers to inflict, that he recommends that they should take place, " *if possible,* in the presence of the plantation-doctor, who should be empowered to limit the extent of punishment." (Vol. ii. p. 219.)

We shall make only one extract more under this head.

" An abuse," observes our author, " at present existing on some properties, is arming the drivers with power to inflict punishment in the field."—" When punishment is inflicted by flogging, the limit should not be extended above 39 lashes, which the overseer is only empowered to inflict by law. It cannot, however, be denied that this limit is often out-done, and by repeatedly punishing offenders the parts become insensible to the *lacerations which tear up the skin.* When that barbarous consequence is arrived at, the infliction of the lash becomes a matter of indifference to the unfortunate Negro, *and new sources of torture must be found out* by which the commission of crime may be checked. It can scarcely be necessary to add, that such a condition of torpor in the parts to which punishment is applied can never be justified on any pretext; and I blush to reflect that White men should be the directors of such disgraceful deeds. Opinions have been given that it would be well altogether to do away the possession of *a large heavy whip* from the driver's hands; and whether we consider the *frightful sound which reaches our ears every minute in passing*

---

* This recommendation is obviously intended by Dr. Williamson to supply some remedy for that principle of colonial law, which excludes the evidence of slaves from being received, in cases affecting persons of free condition.

through estates, by the crack of the lash; or the power with which drivers are provided to exercise punishment; it would be desirable that such a weapon of *arbitrary and unjust authority* were taken from them. It is at present customary to crack the whip to turn out the gangs, at stated hours, to the field. When a Negro seems to be tardy at his work, the driver sounds the lash near him, or *lets him feel it as he thinks proper."** From all this the " *impression* made upon the passenger, who is probably a stranger, *is horrible indeed."*—" Every consideration of humanity and policy points out that the *frequent infliction of the heavy whip to cut up and lacerate severely"* is improper. " *That extreme punishment* †, if awarded, should be only admitted on occasions of very aggravated crime; and it would be well, even under these circumstances, not to inflict it on the single opinion of any individual."

" By abandoning the severity of punishment, unless in cases of very aggravated transgression, the condition of the Negroes will be *immensely* improved. A Negro, subjected to frequent and severe punishment, has an appearance and manner by which he is easily known. *If, in a warm day, we pass by a gang when they are uncovered behind, it is a reproach to every White man to observe in them the recently lacerated sores, or the deep furrows, which though healed up, leave the marks of cruel punishment.* If the management of Negroes can be conducted without such unperishing testimonials of *uncalled-for cruelty,* let not future crimes disgrace us, and let our future humanity towards them compensate for the past." (Vol. ii. pp. 222, 225.)

* Speaking of the driving system, Dr. Williamson observes, in his own obscure way, that " however much it may be the wish of proprietors and attorneys of estates to condemn every step which tends to bear down the Negro incapable of the usual labour of the healthy, it is too true that due consideration is not sometimes given to this point. The interests of proprietors are thus sacrificed to a barbarous policy. On estates this fault is not so common as in jobbing-gangs; but in both the crime is equally culpable, and inimical to their true policy." (Vol. ii. p. 223.)

Now the plain English of this passage we take to be, that on sugar-estates, but still more in jobbing-gangs, the weaker part of the gang are sometimes over-driven, by the impulse of the lash, in order to keep up with the stronger.

† What Dr. Williamson justly calls *extreme punishment* it is nevertheless in the power of every overseer to inflict summarily, at his own discretion, for any fault or for no fault at all.

3. *Miscellaneous Observations.*

General remarks are rare in the work of Dr. Williamson, nine-tenths of it being devoted to medical facts and comments; but such as we have been able to glean, we shall now give.

"The constitution of this island," the Doctor tells us, "in its political establishment, renders it necessary to keep up distinctions in society, *which exclude all persons of Colour from admission into that of Whites.* This exception at first appears extraordinary; but some consideration will point out its necessity." Dr. W. does not, however, inform us of the process by which he arrived at this conclusion, nor does he explain why distinctions in society should attach to colour exclusively.

After speaking of a certain gang of Negroes, who had been purchased at the Marshal's sales, and who, having been seized and sold for payment of their master's debts, had, of course, been forcibly separated from their connections in different parts of the island, he states that medical care was lavished on them in vain. " Depression of mind spread among them."—" They candidly confessed that death was their wish." He then goes on to observe as follows : " Negroes anticipate that they will, upon death removing them from *that* country, be restored to their native land, and enjoy their friends' society in a future state. *The ill-disposed to their masters* will sometimes be guilty of suicide, or, by a resolute determination, resort to dirt-eating, and thus produce disease, and, at length, death. It is often necessary to check that spirit ; and as Negroes imagine that, if decapitation be inflicted after death, the transition to their native country cannot follow, a *humane principle* leads the proprietor to have the head of such a Negro placed in some prominent situation ; and this has been found a salutary mode of deterring the rest from conduct so destructive." (Vol. i. p. 93.)

The Marshal's sales spoken of above, Dr. W. informs us, take place at Spanish Town, which is the seat of the courts of justice for the county of Middlesex ; and he speaks of the practice, though conformable to the existing laws, as being the hardest and the most irreconcileable to a feeling mind that can be conceived. He then indulges in we know not what day-dreams of the early abolition of this power of seizing a Negro, with as little ceremony as an ox or a cask of sugar, and selling him to pay his owner's debts. Six years have since elapsed, and *the practice still exists, in every British slave-colony, in all its horror.*

Dr. Williamson speculates, with equal good nature, on the happy effects which the humanity of colonists and of colonial legislatures will infallibly derive from that, in his view, very questionable measure of policy, the abolition of the Slave-trade : and, we fear, with something of a like result. "'Those who had the barbarity" (it seems there were such) " to count on supplies of slaves from Africa, at the expense of the Negroes already in their possession, *working* THEM *severely, clothing and feeding* THEM *imperfectly,* will now find it their policy to take good care of Negroes for selfish reasons. For some time after I went to Jamaica, *it was customary on a few properties,*" (he does not say on what proportion of those he was acquainted with,) " *not to encourage the rearing of children,* on account of the loss of labour incurred by the mother's confinement, and the time afterwards required in rearing the infant." But now " proprietors and attorneys," (he says nothing of the overseers of non-resident proprietors, by far the most numerous class, and who exercise a more decided influence on the happiness and increase of the Negro population than any other,) but now " proprietors and attorneys will increase their exertions to protect Negroes. On every property, inducements will be held out to encourage the propagation of children, which would be materially promoted by introducing marriage among them." (Vol. i. p. 372.)

This grand and indispensable mean, however, of encouraging population, has not yet been introduced by these proprietors and attorneys, on whose enlightened humanity Dr. Williamson is disposed to place so generous and unbounded a reliance : his warning was given five or six years ago, and has hitherto produced no effect.

III. EVIDENCE OF MR. J———— M————.

J. M. is the son of a respectable tradesman in London, who, wishing to do something for himself, went out, about the beginning of the last year, 1822, to the island of Jamaica, to be a book-keeper on Bushy Park estate, in the parish of St. Dorothy's ; a large estate, belonging to a wealthy and liberal proprietor, and which has the reputation of being managed as well or rather better than usual *. He had no complaint whatever to make against the owner, attorney, or overseer, for any harsh or unkind treatment of himself; but the state of things he found there was so grating to his feelings, that he could not have remained, even though his health had been quite unaffected, which, however, was not the case; and after a few weeks' residence on the estate, he resolved to return to England, in which he met with no opposition. His statement is as follows:

"The slaves on the estate were constantly attended by drivers with cart or cattle whips, which they were in the habit of using as here carmen use their whips on horses; and occasionally one or more slaves were ordered out of the line of work, laid prostrate on the ground, and received a few lashes (from two or three to ten) on their posteriors, for no other offence that he could perceive or ever heard of but that of being indolent, or lagging at their work, or being late. He saw a few working with iron-collars round their necks, connected with each other by a chain; a punishment which, he understood, was usually inflicted for running away, and continued sometimes for several weeks. The huts of the slaves were very indifferent, and almost destitute of furniture. On Sunday they either attended market, or worked in their own grounds; but none went, or were expected to go, to any church or place of worship; nor did he ever see or hear of any instruction, religious or otherwise, being bestowed upon them. Many of the slaves had women living with them as their wives; but as for marriage being used, either as a means of civilization or for any other purpose, he never even heard the word mentioned as it respected them. He understood that the White servants were not allowed to take those women who so lived with particular men; but as for any others, they not only chose and took such as pleased them, but they were expected to do it as a matter of course. Accordingly, he was invited by the overseer to follow the general practice, the very first day he arrived on the estate. In a spare house, kept for the occasional use of persons coming thither for a few days, were women whom he understood to be at the service of whoever came to occupy the apartments, and two of them were spoken of as the children of a former proprietor.

"But little provisions appeared to him to be given to the slaves.

* New Hall Estate (see p. somewhere about 62.) also belongs to him.

Herrings and such fish, rather as sauce than as food, were given them. But they had grounds allotted them, and the Sunday, throughout the year, for their cultivation, with every or every other Saturday out of crop-time (the practice on this head differing) ; and while strong and in good health, this he thought might do very well. But in crop-time (on some estates nearly half the year) they could have very little leisure or inclination to work for themselves, being often greatly fatigued by extra night-work and watching. He understood that, by the law of Jamaica, only thirty-nine lashes could be given at once; but he was told, on the spot, that an overseer could easily, when so disposed, evade it."

The agreement of the three witnesses who have been produced, in all material points, must appear remarkable, especially when it is remembered that they resided on different parts, widely removed from each other, of the same island. Mr. Cooper resided on the north side of the island, the last-cited witness on the south side, and Dr. Williamson, while engaged in plantation-duty, nearly in the centre of it. But we have a fourth witness to bring forward.

IV. EVIDENCE OF THE ROYAL GAZETTE OF JAMAICA.

In the month of January, 1816, there appeared in a periodical work (the same wnich afterwards contained the review of Hall and Fearon, inserted above,) an article entitled " Review of the Reasons for establishing a Registry of Slaves." In that article there occurred the following statement, viz. :—

" It is among the many opprobrious peculiarities of the West India system, that it has created a legal presumption in favour of slavery; so that every person in the islands, who does not boast a pure European descent, is, in all judicial proceedings, assumed to be a slave, until he can prove himself to be a freeman.

" When the importations of African Negroes into our colonies commenced, and for some years after that period, it was, doubtless, the fact that a Black complexion was the certain indication of a servile condition. It was then probably true, without one exception, that every African who was found in a British settlement had been previously reduced by violence to a state of bondage. The

West Indies possess a written and an unwritten law. Their statute-book contains the former : usage, of an origin comparatively modern, is the sole foundation of the colonial *lex nonscripta*. English lawyers would, we apprehend, vehemently dispute the validity of this whole body of traditionary West Indian law ; but difficulties of this kind are not much regarded in the supreme courts of Jamaica or Barbadoes. Relying on customs which have had their birth far within the date of legal memory, it is the doctrine of those tribunals, that the offspring of a female slave necessarily inherit the terrible condition of their mother. In the earlier times of our colonial history, it was, after this principle had been once established, probably true, that Mulattoes as well as Negroes were really in a state of slavery. The mixture of European with African blood could not vary their condition, for that they derived *ex parte materna*, and a White mother of Mulatto children was probably never seen in the West Indian islands. If, therefore, manumissions had never been introduced into our colonies, or if free Blacks had never migrated thither from Great Britain, or other countries, or if a time had never arrived when the importation of the natives of Africa was declared illegal, it would have been strictly true, that a Negro and his remotest posterity were necessarily slaves, and the legal presumption of the servile condition of such persons would have been fairly supported by the real state of the case.

" But the emancipations by purchase, by grant, and by will, have been in use from a time little posterior to the origin of the Slave-trade ; and though during the last nine years it is the admitted fact that large numbers of African Negroes have been liberated in our colonies by the operation of the abolition-laws, yet, strange to say, the courts of justice of every one of the islands continue to act on this cruel legal presumption, with as little attention to the case of manumitted and free Negroes, as if such a class of society had not existed. As the law at present stands, if a White person asserts a right to hold his fellow-creature in perpetual slavery, the burden of proof lies, not on the asserted owner, but on the alleged bondsman. He is required, at the peril of the most severe personal affliction to which men can be subjected in this world, to prove a negative ; to show that he is *not* a slave. In making this proof, he is, by another most iniquitous principle of law, excluded from producing as evidence in his favour the testimony of any of that class of society, the Black or Coloured slave population, to whom alone his right to freedom and the grounds of it may often be known. In Barbadoes, and till the last two years in Jamaica also, he was even unable to summon, as witnesses, the few persons of his own complexion with whom alone he can ever associate, and on his descent from whom his title to liberty frequently depends. If manumitted in the colonies, the loss of the deed of enfranchisement would destroy the only evidence by which his claim could be substantiated. Or should he be among the number of those recently imported from Africa, and restored by the Abolition-act to freedom, his ignorance of the language of the country, to which he has been removed, would of itself prevent his asserting his right to that inestimable blessing ; nay, even if he were born in this happy island, and had the unhappiness to visit our West Indian colonies, he would be liable to be seized as a runaway, and sold into perpetual bondage, for want of a deed of manumission, which, under the circumstances of his birth, he could never have possessed.

"Such is the law, and such also is the daily practice of *British* colonies. It is not merely the individual European claimant, but the State itself, the Crown of Great Britain, as represented by the Executive Government of its colonies, which continually holds the miserable descendants of Africa to this dreadful probation. Let any man take in his hands a file of Jamaica newspapers ; one will scarcely be found without numerous advertisements to the following effect : ' Whereas ——, a man of Colour, *who asserts himself to be free,* has been committed to the public gaol of —— ; notice is hereby given, that unless within —— days the said —— *shall satisfactorily prove his title to freedom,* or shall be claimed by his lawful owner, he will, at the expiration of that time, *be sold for the benefit of the public.*' This we assert to be the exact substance of advertisements which frequently appear in the West Indian Gazettes ; and any man who will take the trouble of looking into them, may satisfy himself of the fact. Nor is this shameless public insult on national justice unsanctioned by law. There is not an island in which this course of proceeding is not expressly authorized, in the case of persons taken up and committed on suspicion of being runaway slaves ; persons, that is to say, who are found in any of the colonies without a master, and without the *legal* proofs of their freedom.

" Nor let it be imagined that such cases are merely supposititious or of unfrequent occurrence. The Royal Gazette of Jamaica itself —the island whose pretensions to the character of justice and mercy, in its legislative acts, are sounded loudly in our ears—need only to be opened, in order to furnish numerous cases of the most aggravated description. We have now before us the file of that paper for 1815 ; and we will give a specimen or two of the evidence which it furnishes. On the 20th May, 1815, we find the following specification of persons confined in the common gaols of the island as runaways :—

" George Thomas, an American ; says he is free, but has no document thereof.

" Samuel Menderson, a Portuguese Creole (no mark, &c.) ; says he is free, but has no document thereof.

" Joseph, a native of St. Domingo (no brand-mark, &c.) ; says he is free : to be detained until he proves his freedom.

" Willian Kelly, a Creole ; says he is free : to be detained until his freedom is proved.

" John Francis ; says he is a native of Curaçoa, and that he is free, but can show no document thereof. There are marks of flogging on his back, which he says he got on board the Hebe frigate.

" Thomas Hall ; says he is free.

" Antonio Belfour, a Sambo ; says he is an American, and that he is free.

" David Barrow, a Samboo ; says he was born at Barbadoes, and that he is free.

" Alexander Antonio ; says he is a Spaniard, and that he is free.

" John Rose, an American Sambo, a sailor ; says he is free.

" Antonio Moralles, a Creole, of the island of St. Thomas ; says he is free, but has no document thereof : came here as carpenter of the schooner Sparrow.

" In the very last paper which arrived from Jamaica, that of the 18th November, 1815, we find the following insertions in the gaol-lists, viz. :—

" John Dixon, a Creole ; says he is free, but has no document thereof.

"John Messar ; says he is free, but has no document thereof.

" Edward Brian Wardins, a Mulatto Creole ; says he is free, but has no other document than a pass signed John Wardins, who says that he is his son, and was born free.

" William Bennett, a Creole; says he is free, but has no document thereof.

" The Gazette of each week exhibits similar and not less numerous instances.

" Here let it be recollected, that all the individuals in the above list (and these form, probably, not a tithe of the cases of precisely the same nature which have appeared in the Royal Gazette of Jamaica during the last year alone) allege that they are free. There is no contrary allegation; they are not claimed by any one as slaves. And yet because they cannot produce documentary evidence of their freedom, (a species of evidence which, perhaps, they never could have possessed, or may have lost,) they are, after a certain time, by the fiat of the Jamaica Legislature, to be sold to the best bidder, precisely as strayed horses or mules who have been impounded, but not claimed, would be sold; and the proceeds of this sale, (the price of blood!) after defraying the gaol expenses, are to be paid into the treasury of the island. Is it possible for an Englishman to contemplate such a state of things as this without horror? and are we not bound, in the sight of God and man, to provide an adequate remedy?"

One would naturally have imagined that so cruel and oppressive a system as this could hardly have been exposed to the view of the British Parliament and public without leading to inquiry at least, if not to some measures of a remedial nature. Seven years, however, have elapsed since the above exposition of this great and crying evil, and no step whatever has been taken to abate it. Charity might suggest that this otherwise unaccountable omission may have arisen from ignorance or inadvertence. West Indians, in this country especially, may not have been aware of the true state of the case, and they may never have seen the article from which the above extract has been taken. There is, however, the most decisive proof to the contrary. On the 19th June, 1816, Mr. Palmer, himself a Jamaica planter, and a leading and influential person among the West Indians, quoted largely from this very article, in a speech of great length and ability which he made in the House of Commons, on an occasion to which we shall hereafter find it necessary to advert. The article was therefore well known to him. But although the very address to the King which Mr. Palmer then moved, in his preface to which he particularly referred to this article, prayed His Majesty " to carry into effect every measure tending to promote the moral and religious improvement, as well as the comfort and happiness, of the Negroes," it is the fact, that the evil in question remains to this day without any effectual redress. To this very day, every Black or Coloured person in the British West Indies is assumed to be a slave, unless he can adduce *legal* proof of his being free.

The evidence of the existence of this principle, not merely in some statute which it might be alleged was obsolete and inoperative, but in active and constant operation, was then drawn from the Royal Gazette of Jamaica. From the same respectable and authentic source we derive the proof, that, up to this day, the same principle continues still to be maintained in law, and acted upon in practice.

From the Royal Gazette of September, 1822, we extract the following notices of persons taken up, and confined as runaways, viz. :—

" In St. Andrew's work-house, Robertson, a Mandingo ; *says he is a discharged soldier, of the second West India regiment, and that he is free.*"

" In St. James's work-house, Joseph Lee, a Creole ; *no apparent brand-mark**: says he is free, but has no document thereof."

In Spanish-Town work-house, Edward Quin, a native of Montserrat, elderly ; no mark : says he is free, but no document."

" In Clarendon work-house, Harry, a Creole ; formerly belonged to Mr. George, who died before the Maroon war (1797) ; has had no owner since : grey-headed."

But what proof is there that these persons were actually sold ? We can adduce no evidence on this point. These persons may, for aught we know, have been able, before the period of their imprisonment expired, to establish their freedom by *legal* proof. But if they were unable to do this, it would only have been following the course prescribed by the law, to sell them, by public auction,

---

* Slaves are commonly marked with the owner's name, like sheep or cattle. The operation is performed with a heated brand.

as slaves. Of this fact the very numbers of the Gazette which have supplied the above extracts furnish evidence. We observe in it the following advertisement :—

" *Westmoreland Work-house, Aug.* 27, 1822.

" Notice is hereby given, that unless the under-mentioned *slave* is taken out of this work-house prior to the 22d October next, he will on that day, between the hours of ten and twelve in the forenoon, be put up to public sale, and sold to the best bidder, agreeably to the work-house law in force, for payment of his fees : viz. John Williams, five feet nine inches and a half high, *no brand-mark ;* says he is a Maroon of Charles-Town, whereof John March, Esq. is superintendant, but which is *supposed to be false,* as he is apparently a foreigner by his speech. He had for some time been seen skulking near Glasgow estate, in this parish."

The following names and descriptions are appended to similar advertisements, viz. :—

" Kingston work-house.—Mary Johnson, an aged Creole ; *no brand-mark* : says she belonged to William Johnson, a Maroon, who has been dead eight years ; since which she has maintained herself."

" Spanish-Town work-house.—Joe, a French Creole ; *no brand :* very black : says he belongs to his father and mother in St. Mary's."

" Clarendon work-house.—Robert, an Eboe, elderly ; belonged to Mr. Macbean, who died some time ago ; has no owner at present."

Now, is it possible to conceive a more tremendous instrument of oppression than the power which the laws of the West Indies convey, to every man in the community, of thus treating as slaves and criminals all whose countenance indicates that they are of African descent, or that they have African blood in their veins ; of imprisoning them as runaways, and of having them afterwards sold into a perpetual bondage, where they, and in the case of women their offspring too, may wear out their wretched lives under the cattle-whip ? As those who take up runaways, and commit them to a work-house, are entitled to a reward for this service, it is obvious that there exists a strong temptation to abuse this power. Any needy ruffian, to whom a few dollars are an object, may first rob a poor wretch of his document of freedom, and then commit him as a runaway. Besides, what a fearful tenure it is by which to hold that precious possession of personal liberty, that if the certificate of it, which a man ought to have in his possession, shall have been lost by accident, or consumed by fire, or stolen, or destroyed by the various insects which abound in tropical climates, he shall be exposed to this appalling risk! But how many free Black and Coloured persons may reside in our islands, or be led to visit them, who may be in this predicament; or who may be ignorant of the requisitions of this cruel law; or who may never have had the means of establishing their freedom by documentary evidence! They may have been born and liberally educated in England. They may have migrated thither from one or other of the numerous provinces of North or South America. They may have been liberated under the Abolition-acts. They may have served in the navy or army of Great Britain, and may have bled in fighting her battles. But if they have either never had such a document of freedom as West Indians have pronounced *legal;* or, having had it, have lost it, they are liable to undergo the merciless and relentless operation of the *work-house law :* and after having laboured for some months, in chains and under the lash, for the benefit of the public, they may then be put up to auction and sold into irremediable bondage, the proceeds to be applied first to the *payment of their fees,* and when that end is answered *(proh pudor!)* to replenishing His Majesty's treasury!!!—Comments would only weaken the effect which the bare statement of such facts is calculated to produce*.

It might be thought disingenuous not to notice in this place the assertion of the Jamaica Assembly, that persons thus taken up as runaways are allowed to establish their liberty by the process called *homine replegiando,* a provison to that effect having been introduced into their last consolidated slave-act. But it may be sufficient to remark, that this process still leaves upon the alleged slave the burden of proving his freedom. To those who wish to examine this question more fully in all its legal bearings, we would particularly recommend a pamphlet, published by Butterworth in 1816, and entitled " A Defence of the Bill for the Registration of Slaves, by James Stephen, Esq., in Letters to William Wilberforce, Esq. ; Letter the Second." The whole subject will be there found fully and most luminously discussed at p. 25—73. The discussion is particularly deserving of the attention of professional gentlemen.

HAVING now detailed the evidence which it was our design to exhibit, in illustration of the more prominent features of Negro slavery, as it actually exists at the present day in our own colonies, and particularly in Jamaica, we shall not exhaust the patience of our readers, nor weaken the effect of the preceding statements, by any lengthened observations of our own. We beg, however, to be permitted to subjoin a few brief remarks.

During upwards of thirty years we have heard many boasts made, both in pamphlets and in parliamentary speeches, of the improvements that have taken place in the condition of the Negro slave; and we were led to indulge a hope, that assertions so confidently made, and so constantly repeated, must have had some foundation on which to rest. On looking narrowly, however, into the facts of the case, we have met with nothing to sustain that hope. We have not been able to discover any *substantial* amelioration in the *nature* of the slavery of the present day, when compared with that which, from the evidence adduced before the Privy Council and Parliament in the years 1788—1791, we learn to have then prevailed. The slavery of both periods appears to us to be identically the same state of existence.

We do not mean to deny that many individual planters, as Mr. Hibbert and others, may have been induced, by the discussions which have taken place, and by their own benevolent feelings, to act a more liberal and indulgent part towards their slaves than formerly. Neither do we mean to affirm that the influence of public opinion, excited by the public agitation of the subject, has had no effect in restraining the abuses of power. What we mean to affirm is, that during the sixteen years which have followed the abolition of the Slave-trade; nay, during the thirty-five years which have elapsed since the condition of Negro slavery has become a topic of controversy in this country, that unhappy state of being has undergone no real or substantial improvement whatever— no improvement, that is to say, which does not depend, we may say wholly, on the dispositions and conduct of the proprietor or of his delegated agent, for the time being.

We admit that various colonial acts have been framed, professing to improve the condition of the slave; but they have been generally inefficient to their professed object, whatever other purpose they may have served. Of the Curates' Act of Jamaica, for example, Mr. Cooper informs us, that he had heard it repeatedly declared, that it was " intended for England, and not for Jamaica;" for, he adds, " *it must have been known* before it was passed, that under the peculiar circumstances existing there, *such a law could have no tendency to improve the condition of the slaves.*" So, with regard to the Register Act of the same island, it is impossible to read it without perceiving that it is wholly inoperative to the ends for which chiefly a registration of slaves was proposed*.

It is true, also, that the leaders of the West India body in Parliament have stood forward, at different times, as the advocates of measures of amelioration.

In 1797, Mr. Charles Ellis moved an address to His Majesty, praying him to call on the different colonial legislatures to adopt such measures as should " appear to them best calculated to obviate the causes which have hitherto impeded the natural increase of the Negroes already in the islands, gradually to diminish the necessity of the Slave-trade, and ultimately to lead to its complete termination ; and particularly, with a view to the same effect, to employ such means as may conduce to *the moral and religious improvement* of the Negroes, and secure to them throughout all the British West India islands *the certain, immediate, and active protection of the law.*"

All the West Indians then in Parliament supported this motion; and although they were considered by the abolitionists as wrong in expecting any effective measures of reform from the colonial legislatures, yet they had at least credit given them for good intentions. It afterwards, however, came out, somewhat awkwardly, that one of the chief movers in this business had held a different language in his confidential correspondence with the local authorities, from what he held in Parliament. There the West Indians professed to make the amelioration of the condition of the slaves and the abolition of the Slave-trade their ultimate objects. In the correspondence, however, which was evidently not intended to see the light, an effort was made to conciliate the acquiescence of the colonists, by

* See " A Review of the Colonial Slave Registration Acts," printed for Hatchard in 1820.

assuring them that the main object of the motion was (not, what it professed, to terminate the Slave-trade, and improve the condition of the slaves, but), as it was expressed by Sir William Young, in a circular letter addressed to influential persons in the West Indies, " *to stop for the present, and gradually to supersede the very pretensions at a future period, to a measure of direct abolition by the mother country*,—a measure which would blast the root of all our settlements of property ; change the foundation of every bequest, loan, and security ; turn every mortgage into an annuity on the lives of the Negroes; institute a general system of foreclosure; and, depreciating our estates, preclude all immediate resources, and ruin every interest."

Nor were the resolutions of the Committee of the West Indian body in London, which accompanied the above letter, less explicit. They state, that " unless some plan of regulation shall be brought forward" by the colonies themselves, " many persons of weight and character," seeing no alternative proposed which is " at all compatible with their ideas of humanity," " will feel themselves under the necessity" of supporting the measures of Mr. Wilberforce. " That, *consequently*, for the joint purposes of *opposing the plan of Mr. Wilberforce*, and *establishing the character of the West India Body*, it is *essential* that they should manifest their willingness to promote actively the cause of humanity, by such steps as shall be consistent with safety to the property of individuals, and the general interests of the colonies." (See House of Commons' papers, ordered to be printed, 8th June, 1804, marked H. Leeward Islands, No. 119)

The West India Committee, or rather their organ, Sir W. Young, having neglected in express terms to enjoin secrecy on their correspondents abroad, these confidential communications were recorded, by the legislatures of St. Vincent's and of the Leeward Islands, as the basis of their proceedings, and as such they made their appearance unexpectedly on the table of the House of Commons.

In consequence of this correspondence, some, but not all, of the colonial legislatures were induced so far to yield a decent compliance with the Royal requisition, as to pass what they called meliorating acts. These, however, have generally, we may say universally, proved a dead letter. The Governor of Dominica,

General Prevost, when called upon by the Secretary of State, Earl Camden, in his circular letter of the 4th of October 1804, to specify what had been their effect in that island, replied, that " from the many years I have passed in the West Indies, and as a resident in most of the colonies, I may venture to represent to Your Lordship the legislature of Dominica as distinguished by the laws it has *passed*, for the encouragement, protection, and government of slaves ; but I am sorry I cannot add, that *they are as religiously observed* as you could wish."—As for " the act of the legislature, ' An Act for the Encouragement, Protection, and better Government of Slaves,' it appears to have been considered, from the day it was passed, until this hour, as a political measure *to avert the interference of the mother-country in the management of slaves.* Having said this, Your Lordship will not be surprised to learn that the seventh clause * of that bill has been wholly neglected."

In other cases the avowal of the motives was not so explicit, but in all the return was NIL. †

In June 1816, Mr. Palmer, an eminent planter of Jamaica, moved in the House of Commons, as chairman of the West India body, another address to the Crown, praying, among other things, that His Majesty would be graciously pleased " to recommend, in the strongest manner, to the local authorities in the respective colonies, to carry into effect every measure which may tend to promote the moral and religious improvement as well as the comfort and happiness of the Negroes." One effect of this motion was to frustrate Mr. Wilberforce's Bill for the Registration of Slaves ; in other words, " to avert the interference of the mother-country in the management of slaves." But there, we fear, its effect has terminated : at least, we are not aware that, during nearly seven years which have now elapsed since this address was moved, the condition of the Negro slave has undergone any substantial amelioration in any of our colonies ; and with respect to the largest of them, Jamaica, the evidence we have now adduced seems to establish the contrary conclusion. But that we may not be accused of

* A clause requiring certain returns to be made for the declared purpose " of securing, as far as possible, the good treatment of the slaves."

† See papers ordered to be printed by the House of Commons, 25th February 1805.

adopting this conclusion on insufficient grounds, we shall specify some particulars, of vital importance to the well-being of the Negro race, in which there is manifestly no real improvement.

1. *The Negroes in Jamaica are still driven at their work by the impulse of the cart-whip, as cattle or horses are driven in this country.*—This fact is undeniable. But let us only consider for one moment all the depressing and brutalizing effects of such a system,—a system which shuts out the Negro from even the pretence to a higher motive for exertion than the fear of the lash, and which extracts labour from him, not in the measure which his strength affords, or his interest prompts, but in the measure which an overseer or a driver may choose to draw from him by the impending terror or the actual infliction of corporal punishment;— let us only consider this one feature of colonial bondage, and we shall at once see enough to account for more than half of its multiplied evils.*

---

* The following description of the driving system has been given by one who was long an eye-witness of its practical operation. It is contained in a pamphlet, published by Hatchard in 1802, entitled " The Crisis of the Sugar Colonies." (p. 8— 13.)

" That West India Slaves, whether French or English, are the property of their master, and transferable by him, like his inanimate effects; that in general he is absolute arbiter of the extent and the mode of their labour, and of the quantity of subsistence to be given in return for it; and that they are disciplined and punished at his discretion, direct privation of life or member excepted : these are prominent features, and sufficiently known, of the state of slavery. Nor is the manner in which the labour of the slaves is conducted a matter of less publicity. Every man who has heard any thing of West Indian affairs, is acquainted with the term *Negro-drivers*, and knows, or may know, that the slaves, in their ordinary field-labours, are *driven* to their work, in the strict sense of the term ' driven' as used in Europe : though this statement no more involves an intimation, that, in practice, the lash is incessantly, or with any needless frequency, applied to their back, than the phrase ' to drive a team of horses' imports, that the waggoner is continually smacking his whip.

" But a nearer and more particular view of this leading characteristic may be necessary to those who have never seen a gang of Negroes at their work.

" When employed in the labour of the field, as, for example, in *holeing a cane-piece*, that is, turning up the ground with hoes into parallel trenches, for the reception of the cane plants, the slaves of both sexes, from twenty, perhaps, to fourscore in number, are drawn out in a line like troops on a parade, each with a hoe in his hand; and close to them, in the rear, is stationed a driver, or several drivers, in number duly proportioned to that of the gang. Each of these drivers, who are always the most active and vigorous Negroes on the estate, has in his hand, or round his neck, from which, by extending the handle, it can be disengaged in a moment,

*2. They are still liable to severe punishments, inflicted in the
most revolting and disgusting manner, at the mere will, uncontrolled by law, of the master, or of the overseer who acts for him.*
—If we contemplate only the *mode* in which *women* continue to be
punished on estates in Jamaica, we shall have another most im-
pressive evidence of the depth of the slave's degradation. The
British Parliament have lately thought it right entirely to prohibit
the flogging of women in this country, in any mode or for any
crime, although that punishment could not have been inflicted
without a regular trial, the finding of a British Jury, and the sentence of a British Judge. But in Jamaica, to this very day, every
overseer retains the power, at his own entire discretion, for any
offence, or for no offence, of exposing in the most shameless
manner, in the presence of the whole gang, the person of every
female, young or old, who is placed under his authority, and of
inflicting on those very parts which it would be deemed in this

a long, thick, and strongly plaited whip, called a *cart-whip*, the report of which is as
loud, and the lash as severe, as those of the whips in common use with our wag-
goners, and which he has authority to apply at the instant when he perceives an
occasion, without any previous warning. Thus disposed, their work begins, and
continues without interruption, for a certain number of hours, during which, at the
peril of the driver, an adequate portion of the land must be holed.

" As the trenches are generally rectilinear, and the whole line of holers advance
together, it is necessary that every hole or section of the trench should be finished
in equal time with the rest; and if any one or more Negroes were allowed to throw
in the hoe with less rapidity or energy than their companions in other parts of the
line, it is obvious that such part of the trench as is passed over by the former will be
more imperfectly formed than the rest: it is therefore the business of the drivers not
only to urge forward the whole gang with sufficient speed, but to watch that all in the
line, whether male or female, old or young, strong or feeble, work as nearly as
possible in equal time and with equal effect; the tardy stroke must be quickened, and
the languid invigorated; and the whole line made to dress, in the military phrase, as
it advances; no breathing time, no resting on the hoe, no pause of languor to be
repaid by brisker action or return to work, can be allowed to individuals: all must
work or pause together.

" I have taken this species of work as the strongest example, but other labours of
the plantation are conducted upon the same principle, and, as nearly as may be practicable, in the same manner.

" In short, with a few exceptions, the compulsion of labour, by the physical impulse or present terror of the whip, is universal; and it would be as extraordinary
in a West India island to see a line of Negroes without a driver behind them, as it
would be in England to see a team of horses on a turnpike-road without a carman or
waggoner."

country an intolerable outrage to expose at all, and which it is indecent even to name, thirty-nine lacerations of the tremendous cart-whip; and the same power, though in a more limited extent, is possessed by every driver on every sugar estate in Jamaica. Let the women of Great Britain hear this, and let them unite their efforts in rescuing their miserable fellow-subjects, the Negro-women of Jamaica, and our other colonies, from this horrid and cruel profanation.

Nor is it merely the power of corporal punishment which is possessed by the master or overseer, but that of adding to it the oppressive imprisonment of the stocks, and that for any length of time, accompanied by hard labour in the field. Here is a subject worthy of the attention of our committees of prison-discipline. Even in this land of freedom, with all our guards of law and magistracy, a free press, and enlightened public opinion, they have found ample room for their benevolent vigilance. Let them not stop there. Let them turn their attention to our slave-colonies. Let them look through the many thousands of places of confinement existing in the West Indies, subject to no legal controul, to no controul, indeed, but that of the owner or overseer of the estate, who is at once the accuser and the Judge, the executioner of the sentence, and the jailer of his victim. Let them examine the stocks, and the bolts, and the fetters, and the chains, and the stripes which await his judgement or caprice, and say whether there be not here a new field worthy of their best exertions.

We have supposed, in what we have said under this head, that the overseer, in the punishments he inflicts, confines himself strictly within that measure of severity which the letter of the law permits him to exercise. But the peculiarity of colonial jurisprudence, to which we shall next advert, serves almost wholly to absolve him from any obligation to make the law the rule of his conduct in the administration of plantation-discipline, and renders almost every attempt to limit the exercise of his authority vain and illusory.

3 *In Jamaica and the other islands the evidence of slaves is still wholly inadmissible, not merely in cases implicating their owner, but in all cases whatsoever, whether civil or criminal, affecting persons of free condition.*—Any White man may inflict not only thirty-nine but three hundred and ninety lashes on a

slave; he may even murder the slave outright; yet, if the crime be not committed in the presence of other persons of free condition willing to testify against him, he is secure from punishment. A thousand other slaves may have been present, but not one of the thousand would be permitted to offer his testimony in a court of justice against the criminal. The Jury would not even be allowed the opportunity of judging of the credibility of his evidence. The mere circumstance of his being a slave would be at once an insuperable bar to his statements being heard. His evidence would be wholly inadmissible. It is equally so in all civil causes, even when the suit involves a question of personal freedom.

It is unnecessary to point out the enormities which must result from such a system. About 345,000 inhabitants of Jamaica, for example, are thus shut out, by the operation of this universal principle of colonial law, from any fair hope of obtaining legal redress for any injury, whether civil or criminal, which they may sustain from any one of the privileged order, amounting, perhaps, to a fifteenth or twentieth part of the whole population; while the persons composing that order have this further pledge of immunity, that it is their common interest to discourage and defeat any attempts, on the part of the slaves, to obtain the efficient protection of magistrates or of courts of justice.

4. *The slaves in Jamaica and other colonies are still regarded by the law, and treated, in point of fact, not as human beings, but as chattels; and, as such, are liable to be seized and sold for the debts of their master, with as little ceremony as a horse or a cart, or a piece of furniture, would be seized and sold in execution in this country.*—Much has been said of the excessive cruelty of this practice even by West Indians. Bryan Edwards has eloquently exposed the many miseries which it produces to the slaves: he even brought a Bill into the British Parliament about 1795, which passed into a law, for removing the impediments it was alleged our statute-book threw in the way of a remedy being applied to the evil by the humanity of the colonial legislatures. Nearly thirty years have since elapsed, and notwithstanding the removal of all impediments; notwithstanding the eloquent denunciations of Bryan Edwards; notwithstanding the undivided support he received from the whole West India body in Parliament; not a single attempt has yet been made, in any one

colony under the British Crown, to remedy the evil. The nearest and dearest relations may still, by the ordinary process of law in civil suits, be torn asunder and separated for ever, dragged from their homes and their families, and sold even into a distant colony. —Great Britain has abolished the African Slave-trade. Even the West Indian planters, who strenuously fought its battles to the last, now join in reprobating its iniquity. But is there any thing in the African Slave-trade which can exceed in horror the practice in question,—a practice, too, specifically sanctioned by the colonial laws,—a practice not of rare and occasional, but of constant and almost daily, recurrence, and which takes place openly and publicly in the chief towns of our colonies ? In our eagerness to induce other nations to abolish their Slave-trade, let us turn our eyes on the abominations of our own.

It seems unnecessary to point out how much the evil of this detestable principle of law must have been aggravated by the pecuniary difficulties under which the West India planters have been labouring, by their own admission, for many years past; and how intensely its pressure on the wretched slaves must be augmented at this present moment by the acknowledged increase of those difficulties.

5. It is a further proof of the hitherto unmitigated degradation of the African race in Jamaica and our other colonies, that, as we have already shown, *a black skin, or even the visible tinge of African blood in the countenance, furnishes a legal presumption of slavery, and exposes the unhappy individual, who cannot repel that presumption by legal evidence, to all the pains and penalties of a cruel and interminable bondage.* But on this point, after what we have said above (p. 68—75), we need not now enlarge.

6. Besides this, *nothing has been done during the last thirty years to promote the gradual manumission of the slave-population, or to remove the obstructions which impeded it ; but, on the contrary, those obstructions have in some instances been materially increased.*—While in the colonies of Spain and Portugal, and particularly of the former, the manumission of slaves has been liberally encouraged ; in our own colonies, it has every where met with discouragement, and in some of them the infatuated policy of the local authorities has even imposed heavy fines on manumissions. The happy effects of the more liberal policy of Spain are visible

even in Cuba, notwithstanding the immense importations of new Negroes which have taken place of late years into that island. But in all the other colonies of Spain, where these importations had ceased, it has issued at length in the almost entire extinction of Negro slavery, and that without any convulsion, nay, without loss to the master or injury to the slave. *

* We annex the substance of a statement on this subject, which has recently been laid before the public. It is to the following effect :—

In the Spanish American possessions it has always been the established practice to encourage manumissions. A slave had a right by law to his freedom, as soon as he could repay to his master the sum he had cost. In order to enable the slave to do this, he was not only allowed the undisturbed enjoyment of the Sabbath, either for rest or for religious purposes, or for his own emolument, as he might like best, but he was allowed also one day in the week for the cultivation of his provision-grounds ; his master being entitled to the labour of the other five. As soon, however, as the slave, by his industry and frugality, had accumulated the fifth part of his value, it was usual for the master, on being paid that amount, to relinquish to the slave another day of the week, and so on until he had repaid the whole of his original cost, and thus became altogether free. He continued, however, in some cases, during the days which were his own, and even after his complete emancipation, to labour for hire in his master's service. By this process, not only was the master's capital replaced without loss, but a peasantry was formed around him, which had learned by experience the happy effects of industry and frugality, and were therefore industrious and provident. Notwithstanding this liberal policy, the enfranchised slaves have never been known in the Spanish possessions to rise against their former masters, or to excite those who were still slaves to seek any other method of deliverance than they themselves had pursued ; whilst they formed, by their number and hardihood, a valuable means of defence from foreign aggression. In consequence of this admirable system, the whole Negro population of the Spanish possessions were so rapidly approximating to emancipation, that about the year 1790, the number of free Blacks and people of Colour somewhat exceeded, in all of them, the number of slaves. Since that time, in Cuba alone, in consequence of the immense importations from Africa into that island, has this proportion been diminished ; but even there the free Black and Coloured population amounts to from a third to a half of the number of the slaves. In the other trans-Atlantic possessions of Spain their number has gone on progressively increasing, until now slavery can hardly be said to have an existence there. And this happy consummation has been effected without any commotion, and with the ready concurrence of the master, who has not only not been a loser, but a gainer, by the change. How opprobrious to Great Britain is the contrast which this system exhibits to that of our colonies !

The happy effects of this admirable mode of manumission are well illustrated in the following extract from Humboldt's Travels :

" We observed with a lively interest the great number of scattered houses in the valley inhabited by freedmen. In the Spanish colonies, the institutions and the manners are more favourable to the liberty of the Blacks than in the other European settlements. In all these excursions we were agreeably surprised, not only at the progress of agriculture, but the increase of a free, laborious population accustomed

Now, if it be not intended by the local legislatures that the state of slavery which now exists in the English colonies shall be perpetual, and that it shall be handed down as the inheritance of the Negro race from age to age, how happens it that not one step has yet been taken by them for relaxing the chains of so many thousands of our fellow-subjects ?—Let it not be forgotten that in the year 1792 Mr. Dundas (afterwards Lord Melville), whose regard for West Indian interests no one has ever questioned, announced his intention of proposing a plan for extinguishing the bondage of our colonies. His plan was simply this, that all children who should be born in the West Indies after a fixed day (the 31st Dec. 1799, we believe,) should be free, and, being free, should be educated by the masters of the parents, and, when arrived at such a degree of strength as should qualify them for labour, should work for five or for ten years, or whatever period it might be, for the payment of the expense of their previous education and maintenance. Thirty-one years have

to toil, and too poor to rely on the assistance of slaves. White and Black farmers had every where small separate establishments. Our host, whose father had a revenue of 40,000 piastres, possessing more lands than he could clear, he distributed them in the valley of Aragua among poor families who chose to apply themselves to the cultivation of cotton. He endeavoured to surround his ample plantations with freemen, who, working as they chose either on their own land or in the neighbouring plantations, supplied him with day-labourers at the time of harvest. Nobly occupied on the means best adapted gradually to extinguish the slavery of the Blacks in these colonies, Count Torur flattered himself with the double hope of rendering slaves less necessary to the landholders, and furnishing the freed men with opportunities of becoming farmers. On departing for Europe, he had parcelled out and let a part of the lands of Cura. Four years after, at his return to America, he found on this spot, finely cultivated in cotton, a little hamlet of thirty or forty houses, which is called Punta Zamuro, and which we afterwards visited with him. The inhabitants of this hamlet are nearly all Mulattoes, Zumboes, or free Blacks. This example of letting out land has been happily followed by other great proprietors. The rent is ten piastres for a vanega of ground, and is paid in money or in cotton. As the small farmers are often in want, they sell their cotton at a very moderate price. They sell it even before the harvest; and the advances thus made by rich neighbours, place the debtor in a state of dependence, which frequently obliges him to offer his services as a labourer. The price of labour is cheaper here than in France. A freeman working as a day-labourer (Peor) is paid in the valleys of Aragua and in the Llanos four or five piastres a month, not including food, which is very cheap on account of the abundance of meat and vegetables. I love to dwell on these details of colonial industry, because they prove to the inhabitants of Europe, what to the enlightened inhabitants of the colonies has long ceased to be doubtful, that the continent of Spanish America can produce sugar and indigo by free hands, and that the unhappy slaves are capable of becoming peasants, farmers, and landholders."

since passed, and we seem further removed from such a consummation at the present moment than we were at that period. Matters, on the contrary, have been getting worse : the local authorities have not only adopted no active measures to promote manumissions, but they have added to the impediments which before existed : they have been so far from empowering slaves, as in the Spanish colonies, to demand their freedom, when by their industry and frugality they have acquired the means of purchasing it, that they have even discouraged, in various ways, voluntary manumissions of meritorious slaves by their masters.

In May 1801, an act was passed in Barbadoes to increase the fines on manumissions from 50*l.* to 300*l.* on each female manumitted, and to 200*l.* on each male. In July 1802, the legislature of St. Kitts imposed a fine of 500*l.* currency on the manumission of slaves born in the island, to be increased to 1000*l.* in the case of slaves not born in the island. In some of the other islands fines of inferior amount were imposed ; and in the Bermudas an act was passed to prohibit emancipation altogether, and to prevent persons of Colour being seised of real estate :—and all these acts received the Royal assent ! Such has been the spirit of colonial legislature even at a recent period !

7. But let us further look at the moral condition of our slave-colonies, and we shall be better able to judge of the real progress of improvement as contrasted with the boasts to which we have alluded. *The marriage of slaves has not yet been legalized in Jamaica or in any one of our slave colonies. The most unrestrained licentiousness prevails, almost universally, on estates, among all classes whether White or Black. The face of society presents, with few exceptions, one unvarying scene of open and promiscuous concubinage and prostitution. The Christian Sabbath, instead of being a day of rest and religious observance, continues to be the universally authorized market-day, and in almost all the colonies, and especially in Jamaica, a day of compulsory labour for the slaves ;* —we say *compulsory labour,* for though they may not be actually *driven* in their provision grounds, on the Sunday, yet they are compelled to cultivate them on that day on pain of starving ;—they toil under the lash for six days in the week, and during the time of crop for six days and three nights, making nine days labour in

the week for a great part of the year ; and yet they are denied the rest of the Sabbath :—they must toil on that day also, or starve.

And while in our colonies the Negro slaves are denied the Sabbath as a day of repose or devotion, in the colonies of Spain and Portugal the conduct pursued is widely different. There, the Sabbath is appropriated in the case of the slaves to rest or religious observances, and another day in the week is regularly allowed them to cultivate their grounds, or otherwise to be employed for their own benefit. The contrast is striking and opprobrious !

When we take this circumstance into view, and when we connect with it the fact of the non-institution of Marriage, and the open and avowed profligacy of manners which prevails in Jamaica, for example ; and when we take into the account, moreover, the driving system, and the arbitrary power of punishment placed in the hands of the Whites, can we wonder that the Negro population should be decreasing in most of our colonies, and especially in those where sugar is extensively cultivated ? * If the human race could increase under such circumstances, it would be contrary to all our received notions of the tendency of the moral government of God. A blight must accompany a system so directly at variance with his known will. His displeasure must rest upon it.

To look also for the effectual communication of religious instruction to the slaves by their masters, under such a system, must be considered as hopeless. We have seen, indeed, striking effects produced by the labours of Missionaries, among the slaves, in several of our islands; but the attempts of these Missionaries have this advantage over any attempts which the masters themselves might make, that they are not rendered abortive, in the very outset, by the glaring inconsistency, which even the slaves themselves must be struck with, of having Christianity offered them by men whose system of proceeding is a flagrant outrage of its most sacred obligations.

Before the planters can hope to succeed in any efforts they may make to convey religious instruction to their slaves, they must, at least, begin by giving them the Sabbath.

We purposely omit many other circumstances in the legal condition of the Negro slave, which tend to aggravate the hardship of his condition, from a fear of too much swelling the present pam-

See supra, p. 30, note.

phlet. We allude to such circumstances as these. He is debarred the common right of self-defence, if the person assaulting him be a White : death, or some other severe punishment, is denounced against him for striking, or attempting to strike, struggling with, resisting, or opposing any White person. He is subject not only to the general criminal law, but to a peculiar penal code of extreme harshness and severity : for example, he is liable to suffer death for obeah or witchcraft; he is liable to death, or dismemberment, for running away; he is liable to thirty-nine lashes for drumming, dancing, drinking, using insolent language or gestures, &c. We will not, however, dwell on this part of the case at present, enough having been brought forward to establish our general position respecting the still unmitigated severity of colonial bondage.

Now, after this view of the subject, when we read again the motions of Mr. Charles Ellis in 1797, and of Mr. Palmer in 1816, (both planters of eminence in Jamaica,) calling upon His Majesty, in grave and set terms, to take measures for promoting " the moral and religious improvement, as well as the comfort and happiness of the Negroes," in what light are we compelled to regard such motions? We should be glad, at least, to learn how many of the West Indian gentlemen who supported those motions, have done what in them lay to promote " the moral and religious improvement, as well as the comfort and happiness of their slaves ;" —how many of them have secured to their own slaves (for this, at least, was in their power)the undisturbed enjoyment of the Sabbath as a day of rest, by giving them the same time, on other days, for the culture of their grounds ;—how many of them, also, have made Sunday, on their own estates, a day of religious worship and instruction. We should further be glad to learn, what efforts they have made to prevent the profanation of that day by public markets and forced labour; —what measures they have adopted for repressing, on their own estates, the shameful irregularities which have been shown so universally to prevail ;—what substitute they have found for the *driving* system ;—and what effective restraints they have imposed, in their own cases, on the tremendous power possessed by overseers. Let them show what they themselves have done in these respects, before they can hope to derive any credit from the barren generalities of a parliamentary address ; which whatever may have been its real purpose, has produced no beneficial results to the Negro population.

We admit that the legislature of Jamaica has passed an act appointing curates for the instruction of the slaves, and giving these curates salaries; but still the slaves have no Sabbath. We also admit that many of the slaves have been christened; but still they have no Sabbath. The very men who vaunt that Curates' Act and those christenings, as a proof of their zeal for Christianity, still deny to their slaves the Christian Sabbath. This fact speaks for itself.

We shall abstain from any further observations on the present occasion, although the subject is very far indeed from being exhausted. But we are anxious, before we conclude, to take this opportunity of calling upon influential West Indians in this country, and especially upon such of them as sit in either House of Parliament, to consider dispassionately the facts we have brought before them, and to ask themselves whether they have done their duty in permitting a state of things, so repugnant to every principle of humanity and justice, to continue so long unmitigated and unredressed. It is surely worthy of such men as Lord Darlington, Lord Harewood, and Lord Holland, not to mention the numerous West India planters and merchants in the lower House of Parliament, to come forward to investigate and reform the abuses of a system which their high names have served, in some measure, to rescue from merited reprobation. To the last-mentioned nobleman, in particular, we would make our appeal, in the confidence that it will not be made in vain. He stands pledged to the African race, not merely by the hereditary obligations which are attached to the revered name of Fox,—not merely by the engagements which he early entered into, and has often renewed in the face of the country, —not merely by the liberal principles which he professes on all occasions to be the guides of his public conduct;—but, above all, by the circumstance that he is himself a planter, and derives a part of his revenue from the cruel and debasing bondage which we have here attempted to delineate. It seems, therefore, peculiarly incumbent on him to take a leading part in instituting an inquiry into its nature and effects, and in applying, without delay, a remedy to its evils.

We would also remind those distinguished friends of justice and humanity in both Houses of Parliament, (our Gloucesters, Grenvilles, Greys, Lansdownes, and Harrowbys; our Wilberforces, Smiths, Cannings, Broughams, and Mackintoshes,) who have toiled so ardently in the cause of the wretched African, that a great duty devolves upon them; and that to them will the public, when their eyes are fully opened to the enormity of the system which prevails in our slave colonies, naturally look for the zealous and consistent prosecution of the principles which animated them in their struggles to suppress the Slave-trade.

But let the public also do their duty. Let them strengthen the hands of their leaders by a general, distinct, and concurrent appeal to the Legislature on this momentous subject. If, through their supineness in making their wishes known, the dreadful evils of colonial bondage should be indefinitely prolonged, will not the guilt become theirs? They cannot plead ignorance of the existence of these evils. Proof has been produced, sufficient to satisfy every reasonable man, that at least a parliamentary investigation is indispensable. Let them then unite in calling for such an investigation, and for such remedial measures as that investigation may show to be requisite. And let them remember, to stimulate their efforts, that at present, they (the British public) do not only tolerate this system, but they actually support it. It could not exist for a single year, but for the aid of the public purse; which, to the extent of two or three millions, is, at this moment, annually expended in bolstering up this fabric of iniquity. But it cannot last. Such a combination of impiety and licentiousness, of oppression and cruelty, of war with all human sympathies, and contempt for all divine laws, cannot continue to meet with countenance and support in this country. It only requires to be known and appreciated, in order to be effectually reformed. If we could for a moment anticipate a contrary result, we should tremble for our country. If, after these practices are known, we should connive at their continuance, nay, if we do not do our best to suppress them, we shall be justly chargeable, in the sight of the Almighty, with all their turpitude and criminality.

But what, it may be asked, are the practical measures it is proposed to adopt? On these we may think it necessary hereafter to address the public. In the mean time our object is simply to expose the enormity of the evils of Negro slavery, with a view to excite the attention of the public, and, through them, of Parliament to the subject. On the wisdom and justice of Parliament we place an implicit reliance. Let the evils be only examined and ascertained, and we cannot doubt that appropriate remedies will be discovered and applied. Neither can we doubt that, in applying them, a due regard will be paid to whatever claims West Indian planters may have on the liberality of the nation.

The present publication, it seems right to mention, has originated with an association at Liverpool, formed for the express purpose of employing all lawful and prudent means for mitigating and finally abolishing the state of slavery throughout the British dominions. Similar associations are already formed in the metropolis and in other parts of the United Kingdom. But it became Liverpool, long the deepest in the guilt of the Slave-trade, to come forward the first to protest against the perpetuation of the original injustice of that criminal traffic, in the persons of the descendants of its earlier victims. Such associations, we trust, will be multiplied in every corner of the realm, and will never intermit their united and strenuous efforts, until by exposition, petition, remonstrance, and every legal method of intervention, they wipe out this foul stain from the character of their country, and deliver themselves from all participation in a system which, as has now been demonstrated, involves the violation of every acknowledged principle of the religion of Christ.

THE END.